# ICONS

Front cover: *Lustre Creme, 1969*
Back cover: *Revlon, 1964*
Endpapers: *Alamac, 1966*
Facing title page: *Fresh Start, 1966*
Inside back page: *Hanes, 1968*

All images are from the Jim Heimann collection unless otherwise noted.
Any omissions for copy or credit are unintentional, and appropriate credit will
be given in future editions if such copyright holders contact the publisher.

**Dates in captions refer to the year of the advertisement's publication and not
necessarily the year in which the product was manufactured.**

To stay informed about upcoming TASCHEN titles, please request our magazine
at www.taschen.com/magazine or write to TASCHEN, Hohenzollernring 53,
D-50672 Cologne, Germany, contact@taschen.com, Fax: +49-221-254919.
We will be happy to send you a free copy of our magazine which is filled with
information about all of our books.

© 2007 TASCHEN GmbH
Hohenzollernring 53, D-50672 Köln
**www.taschen.com**

Design and editorial coordination: Stephen Schmidt / Duuplex, San Mateo
Design assistant: Belinda Cheng, Redwood City
Production: Morgan Slade, Los Angeles
Project management: Barbara Huttrop, Cologne
German translation: Henriette Zeltner, Munich
French translation: Alice Pétillot, Charenton-le-Pont
Multilingual production: www.arnaudbriand.com, Paris

Printed in Italy
ISBN 978-3-8228-4935-4

# Social Evolution & Hemline Revolution

## By Laura Schooling

The decade was known as the Swinging Sixties, and it's easy to understand why. There was the Summer of Love, the sexual revolution, and the Whiskey A Go-Go—America's first disco. The world was experiencing a cultural and political shift, swinging from the conservative stronghold of the 1950s to a youth-led counterculture revolution. The unimaginable became reality, resulting in a collective gasp as a man walked on the moon and a president was assassinated. As the Western world struggled to define itself, the fashion world seemed to do so with whimsical ease. In a decade that produced panty hose, the topless bathing suit, and the miniskirt, it is clear that above all else fashion was in full swing.

On a progressive rise since the late fifties, hemlines were the barometer of the decade's progress; as skirts got shorter, the scope of what was culturally acceptable grew wider. Jacqueline Kennedy's pillbox hats and Doris Day's pastel skirt suits were quickly becoming icons of the old guard. 1960 brought the release of BUtterfield 8 and The Apartment. These sexually charged films earned their fair share of scandal and criticism for open displays of pre- and extramarital affairs, but they also won immense acclaim. Elizabeth Taylor received her first Oscar for her role as a call girl, and The Apartment was named Best Picture of the Year. Men also had no shortness of virile role models. 1962 introduced the world to the dashing James Bond and his lifestyle of fast cars, beautiful women, and bespoke suits. Steve McQueen's tough demeanor had an equally effective way with the ladies. His working-class background and affinity for turtlenecks led the press to call him the "King of Cool." With sexuality bubbling into the mainstream, it seemed only fitting that the first year of the decade introduced America to the birth control pill.

What was projected on-screen was also reflected in fashion magazines. Gone were the upturned noses of socialite models, and replacing them were fresh-faced oddities who embodied change. Their names were as unique as their looks—Twiggy was the perpetual doe-eyed poster girl of mod; Jean Shrimpton possessed a womanly figure with unshakable confidence; and Veruschka was pure, unbridled sexuality, as witnessed when she played herself in Blowup, Michelangelo Antonioni's 1966 tribute to fashion photographer David Bailey. Models were more than just lovely silhouettes; they were as renowned for their personalities as their figures, and each projected a superstar lifestyle. And with TV sets becoming regular living-room fixtures, models were no longer silent images, but celebrities to be heard and emulated.

If sixties fashion had a capital city, it was undoubtedly London. Its dominant youth culture and exploding music scene inspired some of the most influential fashion to date. Renowned for censoring a hip-shaking Elvis in the fifties, The Ed Sullivan Show provided American kids their first glance at The Beatles in 1964 and the forthcoming British Invasion. British TV shows like Ready, Steady, Go and Top of the Pops gave viewers an unparalleled look at bands like The Who, The Rolling Stones, and The Animals, sending fans out to buy their records as well as their shaggy haircuts and slim-fitting trousers at the trendy boutiques dotting London's

Top: *Riviera, 1969*    Bottom: *Lee Jeans, 1968*

Carnaby Street and Kings Road. Sidewalks transformed into runways as kids hit the pavement modeling the latest fashions. Parisian couture no longer predicated the trends; innovation was born on the street. Mary Quant's Bazaar produced some of the most influential looks, and by the mid-sixties she'd created a hemline revolution with the miniskirt. Quant, with her signature five-point Vidal Sassoon haircut, was the originator of and spokesperson for the "London Look." But popularizing the miniskirt is equally credited to André Courrèges, who brought the item to his 1965 runway.

For the first time, youth fashion was not modeled after what adults were wearing. Baby boomers were reaching their teen years and they wanted a unique identity, which often meant borrowing from their own preteen closet. Courrèges popularized Mary Jane shoes, typically worn by children, while Quant's Ginger Group line featured childlike gingham, Peter Pan collars, and short shift dresses. Beauty trends were similarly girlish, with big, exaggerated eyes and pale or nude lips. The natural look was in—wearing makeup that made you look as if you weren't. While this meant looking perfectly pale in England, the opposite was emanating from California, where fashion was all about the surf culture. Bronze skin glowed with sunstruck hair inspired by Gidget, America's favorite surfer girl, and the easy pop anthems of the Beach Boys. Bikinis, paired with short cotton shorts and flower-patterned shift dresses, were perfect for lounging on the sand. Boys wore Hang Ten board shorts, introduced in 1962, often paired with Hawaiian-print and striped cotton short-sleeved shirts.

The commercial release of the Boeing 707 in 1955 turned the sixties into a jet-set playground. The international art intelligentsia used Andy Warhol's Factory as party headquarters. Warhol pretended to eschew the trappings of fashion, but he surrounded himself with some of the most fashionable stars of the time, such as Edie Sedgwick, Mick Jagger, and John Lennon. Ironically, it was Warhol's work and the Pop Art movement that would be picked up and reflected in popular fashion. Warhol elevated silk-screening to high art. With an affinity for uniformity and repetition of base colors, it was no wonder he counted André Courrèges as his favorite designer. Courrèges' 1965 all-white collection was meant to be a futurist look at the year 2000. That same year Yves Saint Laurent took the bold simplicity of Courrèges and added geometric color blocks, inspired by the painter Piet Mondrian, to create one of the decade's most recognizable designs. His square-cut shift dress with distinctively simple color-blocks was widely copied. In 1966 the designer opened his Rive Gauche boutique, famous for its simplistic, androgynous designs like Safari suits and slim-fitting tops paired with tights or hip-hugging trousers. That same year he created Le Smoking—in essence, the female's answer to the tuxedo. Just as the public began to soften toward the miniskirt, it was once again up in arms over the pantsuit. Forbidden in formal settings and the workplace, trousers would become de rigueur for the youth set by the decade's end. Hands down, the most scandalous fashion development of the sixties was thanks to Los Angeles–based designer Rudi Gernreich and his revolutionary experiments with nonstructured, jersey swimwear. His 1964 monokini, a topless bathing suit famously modeled by his muse Peggy Moffitt, achieved real shock—the kind with staying power.

Technology was rapidly improving, perfecting man-made fabrics like nylon and PVC. This allowed clothes to be formfitting without clinging to the body.

Bottom: *Leslie Hornby, 1968*    Top: *Angel Face, 1960*

The sixties also spawned the invention of panty hose, which liberated women from the garter belt. New machines gave manufacturers the ability to mass produce lines of clothing, filling store racks with the latest looks at affordable prices.

1967—the Summer of Love—was the height of the sixties' social and aesthetic revolution, and the cultural attitudes that developed maintained their intensity through the end of the decade. Handcrafted clothes turned heads, as did the tendency to shed clothes entirely—which many did at Woodstock, the 1969 concert that remains one of the most well-documented events in history. While Western-cut denim had been popularized by fifties rebels like James Dean, late-sixties designers like Levi's and Wrangler reinterpreted the material with embroidery and quilting. The musical *Hair* debuted in 1968, celebrating the longhaired hippie aesthetic and free-love ideals. Boys kept growing their hair, and girls' short crops grew out into long, untamed tresses. Wigs increased in popularity throughout the decade, granting women short, big, or bouffant hair on demand. Afro wigs, like other symbols of ethnicity, were embraced and stylized. With sons and brothers in Vietnam, Western fashion looked to assimilate other parts of the world, introducing a multiethnic look that included Mao jackets, kaftans, Indian scarves, and some of the very first black models. Psychedelic prints were no longer synonymous with psychedelic drugs, inspiring the designs of Emilio Pucci and covering everything and everyone, including the iconic Jackie Onassis.

In a time of unparalleled innovation, sixties fashion was whimsical, youth-driven, and audacious. This emotionally charged decade came to a close with scenes of campus protest and the horrifying Manson Family murders, leaving behind a hodgepodge of styles as dramatic as the era itself. Fashion placed its last stamp on the sixties in 1969, the year of the micro-mini. Hemlines, shortened to the absolute max, closed out a decade so raw with emotion that there was truly nothing left to hide.

Above: *Peter Pan, 1967*

# *Evolution der Gesellschaft &*
# *Revolution der Rocksäume*

Von Laura Schooling

Dieses Jahrzehnt ging als die »Swinging Sixties« in die Geschichte ein:
Es gab den Summer of Love, die sexuelle Revolution und das *Whiskey A Go-Go*
– die erste Disco Amerikas. Die Welt machte einen kulturellen und politischen
Wandel durch, brach aus der konservativen Erstarrung der 1950er-Jahre aus und wurde durch eine von der
Jugend geprägte Revolution der Gegenkultur bestimmt. Das Unvorstellbare wurde Wirklichkeit und die
ganze Welt hielt den Atem an, als der erste Mensch den Mond betrat und der amerikanische Präsident
ermordet wurde. Während der Westen mühsam um ein neues Selbstverständnis rang, hatte die Mode
damit keine Probleme. In einem Jahrzehnt, das die Seidenstrumpfhose, den Oben-ohne-Badeanzug und
den Minirock hervorbrachte, gab es modisch so manche Revolution.

Die seit den späten 1950er-Jahren permanent steigenden Säume waren das Fortschrittsbarometer des
Jahrzehnts: Je kürzer die Röcke, desto breiter das Spektrum dessen, was tragbar war. Jacqueline Kennedys
Pillbox-Hüte und Doris Days pastellfarbene Kostüme hatten schon bald ausgedient. 1960 kamen *Telefon
BUtterfield 8* und *Das Apartment* in die Kinos. Diese sexuell aufgeladenen Filme sorgten für einen Skandal
und ernteten heftige Kritik, weil sie vor- und außereheliche Liebesbeziehungen offen thematisierten. Doch
gleichzeitig erhielten sie auch viel Lob und Anerkennung. So gewann Elizabeth Taylor ihren ersten Oscar mit
der Rolle eines Callgirls, und *Das Apartment* wurde zum »besten Film des Jahres« gewählt. Auch den
Männern mangelte es nicht an selbstbewussten Vorbildern. Im Jahr 1962 schloss die Welt Bekanntschaft
mit dem wagemutigen James Bond, dessen Lebensstil von schnellen Autos, schönen Frauen und Maß-
anzügen geprägt war. Steve McQueens männlich-forsches Auftreten stieß ebenfalls auf große Begeisterung
bei der Damenwelt. Seine Herkunft aus der Arbeiterklasse sowie seine Vorliebe für Rollkragenpullis führten
dazu, dass ihm die Presse den Beinamen »King of Cool« verpasste. Sexualität war bald das große Thema
und da traf es sich gut, dass Amerika im ersten Jahr dieses Jahrzehnts mit der Antibabypille vertraut
gemacht wurde.

Was es auf der Leinwand zu sehen gab, spiegelte sich auch in den Modemagazinen wider. Die arrogan-
ten Models, Marke »Höhere Tochter«, wurden von Individualistinnen mit frischen Gesichtern abgelöst,
die zum Sinnbild dieses gesellschaftlichen Wandels wurden. Ihre Namen waren ebenso einzigartig wie ihr
jeweiliger Look – Twiggy war das rehäugige Idol der Mods, während Jean Shrimpton weibliche Kurven und
ein unerschütterliches Selbstvertrauen besaß. Veruschka verkörperte den puren, zügellosen
Sex – wie der 1966 gedrehte Film *Blowup* beweist, Michelangelo Antonionis Tribut an
den Modefotografen David Bailey, in dem sie sich selbst spielte. Models waren
plötzlich mehr als nur hübsche Kleiderständer. Ihre verschiedenen
Persönlichkeiten waren ebenso berühmt wie ihre Maße und jede führte das
Leben eines Superstars. Nachdem der Fernseher zum festen Bestandteil jeder
Wohnzimmereinrichtung gehörte, waren Models keine stummen Abziehbilder
mehr, sondern Prominente, auf die man hörte und denen man nacheiferte.

Top: *Kleinert's, 1962*    Bottom: *Career Club, 1967*

Wenn es in den Sixties eine Modehauptstadt gab, dann London: Die dortige Jugendkultur sowie die sich explosionsartig entwickelnde Musikszene inspirierten einige der einflussreichsten Modeströmungen überhaupt. Nachdem *The Ed Sullivan Show* noch in den 1950er-Jahren von sich reden gemacht hatte, weil sie einen hüftschwingenden Elvis zensiert hatte, gab sie den amerikanischen Jugendlichen 1964 einen ersten Eindruck von den Beatles, deren weltweiter Siegeszug kurz bevorstand. Britische Fernsehshows wie *Ready, Steady, Go* und *Top of the Pops* ermöglichten es den Zuschauern, Auftritte von Bands wie The Who, den Rolling Stones und den Animals auf eine bisher nie gekannte Weise mitzuerleben. Sie sorgten dafür, dass die Fans loszogen, um sich nicht nur deren Platten, sondern auch gleich deren wilde Frisuren und enge Hosen in den angesagten Boutiquen der Londoner Carnaby Street und Kings Road zu besorgen. Die Bürgersteige wurden zu Laufstegen, wo die Kids die neuesten Modetrends zur Schau stellten. Von nun an bestimmte nicht mehr die Pariser Couture die Trends – stattdessen wurden die Innovationen auf der Straße geschaffen. Mary Quants *Bazaar* kreierte viele einflussreiche Looks und trat mit ihrem Minirock bis Mitte der 1960er-Jahre eine regelrechte Saumrevolution los. Mit ihrer unverwechselbaren Frisur, dem Five-point-Cut von Vidal Sassoon, war Quant die Erfinderin und Wortführerin des »London Look«. Die Verbreitung des Minirocks verdanken wir allerdings genauso André Courrèges, der ihn 1965 auf den Laufsteg brachte.

Zum ersten Mal war die Mode der Jugend nicht mehr dem nachempfunden, was die Erwachsenen trugen. Die Babyboomer kamen gerade ins Teenager-Alter und sehnten sich nach einer eigenen Identität, was nicht selten bedeutete, dass sie Anleihen aus dem Kleiderschrank ihrer Kindheit nahmen. So brachte Courrèges Mary-Jane-Schuhe in Mode, die ursprünglich nur Kinder trugen, während Quants Label *Ginger Group* auf kindliche Karomuster, Peter-Pan-Krägen und kurze Etuikleidchen setzte. Die Beautytrends waren ebenso mädchenhaft: große, betonte Augen und helle bzw. ungeschminkte Lippen. Ein natürlicher Look war gefragt – das unsichtbare Make-up. In England bedeutete das totale Blässe, während aus Kalifornien der gegenteilige Trend herüberschwappte, da sich die dortige Mode hauptsächlich an der Surfer-Szene orientierte. Bronzefarbene Haut schimmerte zu sonnengebleichtem Haar, wie es Gidget, Amerikas beliebtestes Surfer Girl, und die Beach Boys mit ihren eingängigen Pophymnen vormachten. Bikinis, kurze Baumwollshorts und Etuikleider mit Blumenmustern waren das perfekte Outfit, um sich im Sand zu rekeln. Die Jungs trugen Surf-Shorts von Hang Ten, die 1962 auf den Markt kamen, dazu häufig kurzärmelige Baumwollhemden mit Hawaii- oder Streifenmustern.

Als im Jahr 1955 die Boeing 707 ihre Flüge aufnahm, wurden die Sixties zum Tummelplatz des Jetset. Die internationale Intelligenzija der Kunstszene nutzte Andy Warhols Factory als Party-Hauptquartier. Warhol gab zwar vor, gegen die Verlockungen der Mode gefeit zu sein, umgab sich aber gleichzeitig mit so modebewussten Stars wie Edie Sedgwick, Mick Jagger und John Lennon. Ironischerweise wurde ausgerechnet Warhols Werk und die Pop-Art-Bewegung vom allgemeinen Modetrend aufgegriffen und zitiert. Warhol erhob den Seidensiebdruck zur hohen Kunst. Angesichts seiner Vorliebe für Uniformität und Primärfarben verwundert es kaum, dass er André Courrèges als seinen Lieblingsdesigner bezeichnete. Courrèges' reinweiße Kollektion von 1965 war als futuristischer Ausblick auf das Jahr 2000 gedacht. Im selben Jahr griff Yves Saint Laurent die kraftvolle Schlichtheit von Courrèges auf, ergänzte sie – inspiriert vom Maler Piet Mondrian – durch geometrische Farbblöcke und schuf so eines der bekanntesten Designs jenes Jahrzehnts. Sein gerade geschnittenes Etuikleid mit den typischen Farbflächen wurde vielfach kopiert.

Above: *Cotton, 1968*

1966 eröffnete der Designer seine Boutique *Rive Gauche*, die für ihre schlichten, androgynen Entwürfe berühmt wurde: Safarianzüge und figurbetonte Oberteile, die man mit schmal geschnittenen oder tief auf der Hüfte sitzenden Hosen kombinierte. Im selben Jahr kreierte er auch »Le Smoking« – das weibliche Pendant zum Abendanzug für den Herren. Man hatte sich gerade erst an den Minirock gewöhnt, da sorgte der Hosenanzug für neuen Aufruhr. Auch wenn sie bei offiziellen Anlässen und am Arbeitsplatz noch verpönt waren, wurden Hosen gegen Ende des Jahrzehnts mehr oder weniger zur Uniform der Jugend. Die skandalträchtigste modische Neuerung der Sechziger haben wir allerdings dem in Los Angeles arbeitenden Designer Rudi Gernreich und seinen revolutionären Experimenten mit unverstärkten Jersey-Badeanzügen zu verdanken. So sorgte sein Monokini von 1964, ein Oben-ohne-Badeanzug, den seine Muse Peggy Moffitt auf unvergessliche Weise präsentierte, für einen regelrechten Schock.

Die Bekleidungstechnologie machte ebenfalls rasante Fortschritte und perfektionierte Kunstfasern wie Nylon und PVC. Das ermöglichte eine figurbetonte Kleidung, die trotzdem nicht am Körper klebte. In die 1960er-Jahre fiel auch die Erfindung der Strumpfhose, die Frauen vom Hüfthalter erlöste. Neue Maschinen ermöglichten den Herstellern die Massenproduktion von Kollektionen und füllten die Regale mit den neuesten Trends zu erschwinglichen Preisen.

1967 – das Jahr des *Summer of Love* – bildete den Höhepunkt der sozialen und ästhetischen Revolution – die damals erworbenen, gesellschaftlichen Überzeugungen behielten ihre Gültigkeit bis zum Ende des Jahrzehnts. Handgefertigte Kleidung sorgte genauso für Aufsehen wie die Neigung, sich seiner Kleidung völlig zu entledigen – was 1969 viele in Woodstock taten – ein Konzert, das bis heute als eines der bestdokumentierten Events aller Zeiten gilt. Während Rebellen der Fifties wie James Dean den Denim im klassischen Western-Schnitt populär gemacht hatten, interpretierten Marken wie Levi's und Wrangler das Material nun mit Stickereien und Wattierungen neu. Das 1968 uraufgeführte Musical *Hair* feierte die langhaarige Hippie-Ästhetik sowie das Ideal der freien Liebe. Daraufhin ließen sich die Jungs die Haare wachsen und auch die Mädchen züchteten ihre Kurzhaarfrisuren zu wallenden, ungebändigten Mähnen. Während der gesamten Sixties wuchs auch die Beliebtheit von Perücken, denn sie verhalfen Frauen je nach Lust und Laune im Nu zu kurzem, üppigem oder hoch aufgetürmtem Haar. Afro-Perücken waren wie andere Ethno-Symbole ebenfalls sehr gefragt. Während die Söhne und Brüder in Vietnam waren, bemühte sich die westliche Mode andere Modeströmungen aufzunehmen und kreierte einen multikulturellen Look, der auch Mao-Jacken, Kaftane, indische Tücher und einige der allerersten schwarzen Models mit einschloss. Psychedelische Muster waren nicht mehr nur ein Synonym für bewusstseinserweiternde Drogen: Man sah sie überall, auf den Entwürfen von Emilio Pucci genau wie an der Stilikone Jackie Onassis.

In einer Zeit noch nie da gewesener Innovationen war die Mode der Sixties skurril, jugendlich und gewagt. Dieses stark emotional aufgeladene Jahrzehnt endete in Studentenprotesten und den schrecklichen Manson-Morden. Es hinterließ einen Stilmix, der genauso revolutionär war wie die Ära selbst. Ihren letzten Coup landete die Mode der Sixties im Jahr 1969 mit dem Mikromini. Diese bis zum Gehtnichtmehr gekürzten Säume beendeten ein Jahrzehnt so voller nackter Emotionen, dass es wirklich nichts mehr zu verbergen gab.

Above: *Mavest, 1968*

# Évolution sociale et révolution de l'ourlet

## Par Laura Schooling

Ce n'est pas pour rien que les années 1960 ont été baptisées les « Swinging Sixties » : au cours de cette décennie, le monde occidental a connu l'Été de l'amour, la révolution sexuelle et l'ouverture du *Whiskey A Go-Go*, la première discothèque d'Amérique. Les États-Unis ont vécu un bouleversement culturel et politique qui les a fait basculer du conservatisme forcené des années 1950 à une révolution culturelle menée par la jeunesse. L'inimaginable est devenu réalité : un homme a marché sur la Lune et un président a été assassiné. Alors que l'Occident semble lutter pour trouver son identité, le monde de la mode se définit avec une aisance fantasque. Il donne naissance au collant, au monokini et à la minijupe et se trouve à l'épicentre du séisme culturel des années 1960.

L'ourlet, qui remonte lentement mais sûrement depuis la fin des années 1950, est le baromètre du progrès : à mesure que les jupes raccourcissent, le faisceau des possibles s'élargit. Les toques de Jacqueline Kennedy et les tailleurs pastel de Doris Day sont vite remisés au rang de symboles de la vieille garde. L'année 1960 voit la sortie sur les écrans de *La Vénus au Vison* (*BUtterfield 8*) et de *La Garçonnière* (*The Apartment*). Ces deux films, qui laissent la part belle à la sexualité, ont reçu leur lot de scandale et de critiques pour avoir exposé des liaisons avant et pendant le mariage, mais ils ont aussi remporté un vif succès. Elizabeth Taylor reçoit son premier Oscar pour le rôle de la call-girl et *La Garçonnière* est sacré meilleur film de l'année. Les hommes ne sont pas non plus en mal de modèles virils. En 1962, le monde fait la connaissance du fringant James Bond, de son style de vie débridé fait de voitures rapides, de femmes magnifiques et de costumes sur mesure. Les allures de dur au cœur tendre de Steve McQueen ont un succès tout aussi imparable auprès des dames. Ses origines modestes et son goût pour les cols roulés lui valent le surnom médiatique de « King of Cool ». Alors que le courant dominant est gagné par l'ébullition sexuelle, la première année de la décennie fait aussi entrer l'Amérique dans l'ère de la pilule contraceptive.

Ce qui est projeté sur le grand écran transparaît aussi dans les magazines de mode. Le nez retroussé des mannequins mondains cède la place au minois frais de créatures excentriques qui incarnent le changement. Leurs noms sont aussi uniques que leur allure : Twiggy, la perpétuelle icône *mod* aux yeux de biche ; Jean Shrimpton, toute en courbes et en confiance inébranlable ; Veruschka, un concentré de sexualité qui s'impose lorsqu'elle joue son propre rôle dans *Blowup* (1966), hommage rendu par Michelangelo Antonioni au photographe de mode David Bailey. Les mannequins sont alors plus que des jolies silhouettes : elles sont aussi connues pour leur personnalité que pour leurs mensurations et mènent des vies de vedette. Les plateaux de télévision se changent en salons où l'on cause : les mannequins ne sont plus seulement des images silencieuses mais des célébrités que l'on prend plaisir à écouter, et à imiter.

Si la mode des années 1960 a une capitale, c'est sans doute possible Londres. Sa culture de la jeunesse et l'explosion de la scène musicale inspirent à la mode quelques-uns des plus grands moments de son histoire. Dans l'*Ed Sullivan Show*,

Top: *Clairol, 1969*     Bottom: *National Cotton Council, 1967*

notamment connu pour avoir censuré les déhanchements d'Elvis dans les années 1950, les petits Américains découvrent les Beatles en 1964. C'est le début de la « British Invasion ». Les émissions britanniques comme *Ready, Steady, Go* ou *Top of the Pops* exposent aux yeux des téléspectateurs, comme aucun média auparavant, des groupes comme les Who, les Rolling Stones ou les Animals. Les fans se précipitent dans les boutiques branchées de Carnaby Street et de Kings Road non seulement pour acheter leurs albums mais aussi pour adopter leurs coupes de cheveux longues et leurs pantalons étroits. Les trottoirs deviennent des podiums sur lesquels les gamins exhibent les dernières tendances. Ce n'est plus la haute couture parisienne qui donne le ton, mais la rue. Le *Bazaar* de Mary Quant donne naissance aux looks les plus suivis, jusqu'à ce qu'elle révolutionne définitivement l'ourlet au milieu de la décennie en créant la minijupe. L'autodidacte Mary Quant, avec sa fameuse coupe au bol créée par Vidal Sassoon, est la créatrice et l'ambassadrice du « London Look », même si la popularité de la minijupe doit aussi beaucoup à André Courrèges, qui l'inclut dans son défilé en 1965.

Pour la première fois, la mode des jeunes ne prend plus exemple sur ce que portent les adultes. La génération du baby-boom atteint l'adolescence et revendique sa propre identité, quitte à aller piocher dans sa garde-robe d'enfance. Courrèges généralise les ballerines Mary Jane, les *babies*, tandis que Mary Quant propose vichy, grands cols à la Peter Pan et mini-robes droites dans une collection pour le réseau américain de vente en gros *Ginger Group*. En matière de beauté, la tendance est aussi aux jeunes filles en fleur, yeux exagérément grands, lèvres pâles ou sans rouge à lèvres. Le look naturel est à la mode : il s'agit de se maquiller sans en avoir l'air. Si ce goût pour le naturel s'exprime par une pâleur impeccable en Angleterre, il déclenche la tendance inverse en Californie, alors totalement vouée au culte du surf. Les peaux sont dorées, les cheveux décolorés par le soleil et le sel comme ceux de Gidget, la surfeuse préférée des Américains. La jeunesse se prélasse au son facile des tubes pop des Beach Boys, les filles en bikini, petit short en coton et robe courte à fleurs, les garçons arborant le bermuda de surf Hang Ten, commercialisé en 1962, le plus souvent avec des chemisettes hawaïennes ou rayées.

Le lancement commercial du Boeing 707, en 1955, transforme le monde des années 1960 en gigantesque terrain de jeu pour la jet-set. L'intelligentsia internationale des artistes se retrouve à la Factory d'Andy Warhol qui, tout en prétendant éviter les pièges de la mode, s'entoure des vedettes les plus branchées du moment : Edie Sedgwick, Mick Jagger, John Lennon... L'ironie veut que la mode populaire ait justement retenu et adopté le travail de Warhol et le Pop Art comme référence. Warhol a élevé la sérigraphie au rang de grand art. Son goût pour l'uniformité et la répétition de couleurs primaires le porte tout naturellement à apprécier le travail d'André Courrèges, son couturier favori, dont la collection blanche de 1965 a pour ambition d'être encore futuriste en l'an 2000. La même année, Yves Saint Laurent s'empare de la simplicité audacieuse de Courrèges, y ajoute des blocs de couleur géométriques inspirés du peintre Piet Mondrian, et crée certains des modèles les plus reconnaissables de la décennie. Sa petite robe trapèze à motifs géométriques sera largement copiée. En 1966, le couturier ouvre la boutique Rive Gauche, célèbre pour ses créations simplissimes et androgynes comme ses ensembles tunique pantalon, ses

Bottom: *Allied Chemical, 1968*     Top: *Jane Inwill, 1961*

sahariennes ou son fameux smoking pour femmes . Pour le grand public, qui commence tout juste à accepter la minijupe, c'en est trop : il se révolte contre l'ensemble pantalon. Interdit de soirées et proscrit au travail, le pantalon devient pourtant « incontournable » en quelques années auprès des jeunes. Les esprits évoluent en même temps que les matières et la déclaration de mode la plus scandaleuse de la décennie vient sans conteste du créateur Rudi Gernreich, qui révolutionne le vêtement de bain en développant à Los Angeles le maillot en jersey sans armatures. Son monokini de 1964, un bas de maillot avec des bretelles croisées entre les seins nus, magistralement mis en vedette par sa muse Peggy Moffitt, fait l'effet d'une bombe et laisse l'Amérique paralysée de stupeur.

La technologie progresse rapidement et vient perfectionner les tissus industriels comme le nylon ou le PVC. Les vêtements évoluent pour pouvoir mouler le corps sans l'étouffer. Les années 1960 engendrent aussi le collant, qui libère les femmes du porte-jarretelles. De nouvelles machines permettent aux créateurs de produire des lignes de vêtements en série et de remplir les magasins des dernières tenues tendance à des prix abordables.

L'Été de l'amour, en 1967, marque l'apogée de la révolution sociale et esthétique des années 1960 et l'avènement de comportements culturels qui conserveront leur intensité jusqu'à la fin de la décennie. Les vêtements faits main ont la cote, tout comme l'envie furieuse de ne plus en porter du tout. Beaucoup cèdent d'ailleurs à ce désir de libération au concert de Woodstock, en 1969, comme le montrent une profusion de documents. Le jean brut coupe Western vulgarisé par les rebelles des années 1950 comme James Dean est réinterprété par les designers de la fin des *Sixties* comme Levi's et Wrangler, qui lui apposent broderies et matelassages. La comédie musicale *Hair*, créée en 1968, célèbre l'esthétique hippie et l'amour libre. Les garçons se laissent pousser les cheveux et les petites coupes courtes des filles s'allongent en boucles sauvageonnes. Les perruques, qui offrent aux femmes la possibilité de passer à volonté d'une touffe de boucles rousses à un carré platine, sont de plus en plus en vogue. Les perruques afro, tout comme d'autres symboles d'appartenance ethnique, sont détournées et stylisées. Les fils et les frères d'Amérique se battent au Viêtnam et la mode occidentale ressent l'appel des autres parties du monde : apparaît alors un style multiethnique qui adopte aussi bien la veste à col Mao que le kaftan, le foulard indien ou les tout premiers mannequins noirs. Les imprimés psychédéliques ne riment plus forcément avec les drogues du même nom et inspirent ses fameux motifs au créateur italien Emilio Pucci, qui habille tout et tous, jusqu'à l'icône de la mode qu'est toujours Jackie Onassis.

Surfant sur ces innovations sans précédent, la mode a su se montrer fantasque, audacieuse et à l'écoute de la jeunesse. Cette décennie si chargée en émotions se clôt sur les images des manifestations dans les universités et des assassinats barbares perpétrés par la famille Manson, qui viennent parachever un mélange de genres aussi spectaculaire que l'ont été les années 1960 elles-mêmes. La mode a marqué les *Sixties* d'une dernière empreinte en 1969, avec la « micromini ». Elle ne pouvait trouver point d'orgue plus opportun que ce fameux ourlet, remonté aussi haut que la décence le permet, pour une décennie à l'issue de laquelle rien ne se cache plus.

Above: *Groshire, 1968*

*Cutex, 1960*

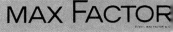

*Max Factor, 1961*

How

to enjoy

the sun

...in style

Redbook

NEW IDEAS
IN FOOD,
FASHION
AND BEAUTY

10 VACATIONS
ON A
BUDGET

5 NEW STORIES
FROM YOUR
FAVORITE
AUTHORS

"Cover Girl does so much for my skin, so beautifully. I love it!" says Cover Girl Marianne Nestor.

# At last! A Cover Girl complexion…
# so <u>natural</u> you can't believe it's make-up!

*Fabulous discovery from Noxzema! Fragrant new Cover Girl covers so naturally, so completely.*
*And it's medicated and antiseptic to help prevent skin problems, improve your complexion.*

*In 3 glamorous shades,*
*3 beautiful compacts*
*$1.50 each plus tax*

New Cover Girl is so light and lovely on your face
. . . so good for your skin besides! Unlike many
make-ups that do nothing for your skin (often even
aggravate skin problems) Cover Girl gives you the
beauty benefits of its special medication.

Smooth on Cover Girl liquid every morning. Touch
up with the pressed powder all day. It's antiseptic
to fight germs on your puff—help prevent skin problems. Helps your skin *look* lovely, *become* lovely.
No wonder it's the make-up of cover girls!

©1961 THE NOXZEMA CHEMICAL COMPANY

*NEW* Cover Girl *MEDICATED MAKE-UP BY NOXZEMA*

Natural
Angel Face

Pink
Angel Face

Picture proof: see how different Angel Face shades can change this beauty's complexion (and yours) to make every fashion color becoming

# Now! You can change your skin

## in any fashion color—with Pond'

Here's the first fashion cosmetic—Pond's new Angel Face! It's the *only* compact makeup with cosmetic-silicones—and it actually lets you wear different skin tones for different fashion colors!

You can choose an Angel Face shade to brighten your complexion . . . another to lighten your complexion . . . another to tone it down. Angel Face makes hard-to-wear fashion colors flattering to you as no other makeup can. Because Angel Face—and no other makeup—has cosmetic-silicones.

This Pond's discovery lets Angel Face change your skin tone naturally, beautifully. Cosmetic-silicones form a protective barrier against skin moisture so Angel Face shades won't darken or discolor.

Nobody's complexion is *quite* perfect, so you'll love the way creamy Angel Face conceals every tiny freckle and flaw . . . gives you the look of a perfect complexion.

Today get two, three or more new Angel Face shades and look lovely in *any* fashion color!

*Angel Face, 1960*

Blushing
Angel Face

Golden
Angel Face

Eyes by Aziza

ne to look lovely

ew *Angel Face*

# buy it...he'll love it!

**EXECUTIVE** men's toiletries
for the man's man from 9 to 5
...the lady's man after six!

New refills
can be
inserted
instantly...
handsome
dispenser
lasts for
years!

$2.50
plus excise tax

"9 TO 5" and "AFTER SIX" colognes
for men; also Pre-Electric & After Shave
lotions—set of any two, $5; single dispenser,
$2.50—handsomely gift-boxed. Refills $2

*Executive*
AFTER SHAVE LOTION

"Everything he needs for masculine good grooming" · EXECUTIVE TOILETRIES, LTD., Santa Monica

W4

Executive Toiletries, Ltd., 1960

# The Best Dressed Men Use

# Duke.

*the greaseless
hair pomade
for men*
that trains and holds
your hair in perfect
place all day long.

*Remember . . .*
women love that
DUKE look!

**75c for the regular size and
$1.25 for the economy size
at your drug counter; or,
send us 90c for the regular
size or $1.50 for the econo-
my size, and we'll send
DUKE to you by return mail.**

*Not too hard . . . not too soft . . . just right!*

ECONOMY SIZE $1.25        REGULAR SIZE 75c

Distributed by *Supreme Beauty Products Company*, 1808 South Michigan Avenue, Chicago, Illinois 60616

*Duke for Men, 1967*

# AVON FOR MEN

# Put your hand over the gray half and see how much younger I look.

**Cover the gray hair in the photo and the years go. Cover the dark hair and the years come clumping back.**

Young/old/young/old/young/old/young/old—it happens every time you shift your hand. Which goes to prove just one thing. Gray hair makes you look older. And dark hair makes you look younger.

But we suspect you've known that all along. Then how come you didn't do something about it before now?

We suspect you know the answer to that one, too.

The embarrassment.

The embarrassment of having to stand in a crowded drugstore and ask for a bottle of women's haircoloring "for-uh-your wife."

The embarrassment of having friends (and unfriends) kid you about it—"Hey, fellows, look —Charley dyed his hair."

And finally, there was the biggest embarrassment of all—the funny feeling that doing something to your gray was too flashy, too "show biz," not for a "regular fellow."

### GREAT DAY ® For Men

Well, let's take the last worry first. Because if we can get you over that one, we have a new product that *solves all the other problems.* (It's called *"Great Day."* From Clairol Research. More about it later.)

### More Men Than You Think

It may have been true ten years ago that only a few actors colored their hair. But since then a

minor, and somewhat surprising, revolution has taken place. Today it's estimated that over 2,000,000 men from all walks of life have broken with tradition and have done something about their gray hair—bankers, farmers, longshoremen, teachers and police officers do it. Without blushing.

They all have one thing in common: they don't want to look old before their time.

### No Embarrassment

Now, finally there's a product designed especially for men—a product that won't embarrass you in any way. Great Day. With Great Day a man can return his graying hair to a soft, rich, natural-looking color in the privacy of his own bathroom, or have it done in any good barbershop. Without any of the worries.

### We Give It To You Straight

Great Day works like a shampoo. Once every two weeks or so, you pour it on—*straight from the bottle.* (No mixing.) Lather it in, let it sit, rinse it off. No complications. Leave it on a few minutes each time, and you color the gray gradually. If you want to take the plunge all at once, just leave it on longer before rinsing.

### Nobody Notices

Great Day doesn't change your natural hair color. It only works on the gray. The change is subtle. Amazingly, even though *you're* very conscious of what you've done, experience has shown that most people don't even notice the difference in color. Only the effect. "Say, Charley, you look great. Did you lose weight or something?"

### Your Pillow Won't Talk

Great Day goes inside your gray hair shafts. So it can't rub off on your collar, or on the pillow. It contains no peroxide in any form. It doesn't harm your hair in any way. (Actually, it leaves your hair in better condition.) It doesn't affect the texture of your hair at all. But just by making it darker, it does make it look somewhat fuller. (Nobody will mind *that* extra benefit.)

Great Day is made by Clairol, the world's leading authority on women's haircoloring. Now, after years of laboratory work and thousands of tests on gray-haired men, Clairol can say, "Hair color so natural only his *barber* knows for sure."* And unless your barber applied it to your hair himself, even *he* won't be absolutely certain.

Muster up your courage a little—and do something about your gray hair.

It's nice to look young.

*TM© 1965, 1966 CLAIROL INC.

great jewel rob

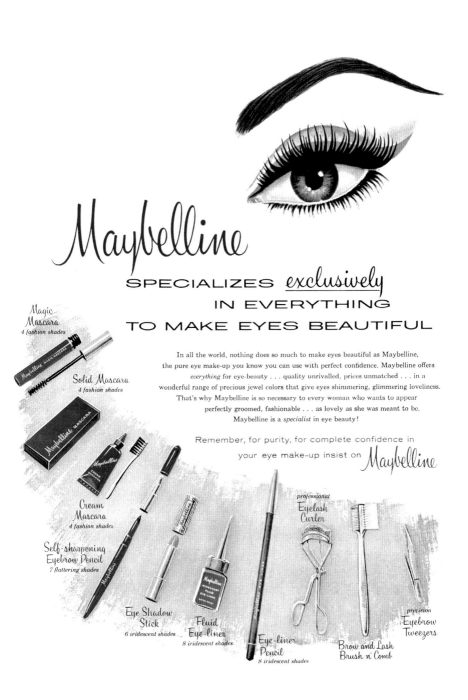

Maybelline

SPECIALIZES *exclusively*
IN EVERYTHING
TO MAKE EYES BEAUTIFUL

In all the world, nothing does so much to make eyes beautiful as Maybelline,
the pure eye make-up you know you can use with perfect confidence. Maybelline offers
*everything* for eye-beauty . . . quality unrivalled, prices unmatched . . . in a
wonderful range of precious jewel colors that give eyes shimmering, glimmering loveliness.
That's why Maybelline is so necessary to every woman who wants to appear
perfectly groomed, fashionable . . . as lovely as she was meant to be.
Maybelline is a *specialist* in eye beauty!

Remember, for purity, for complete confidence in
your eye make-up insist on *Maybelline*

*Magic*
*Mascara*
4 fashion shades

*Solid Mascara*
4 fashion shades

*Cream*
*Mascara*
4 fashion shades

*Self-sharpening*
*Eyebrow Pencil*
7 flattering shades

*Eye Shadow*
*Stick*
6 iridescent shades

*Fluid*
*Eye-liner*
8 iridescent shades

*Eye-liner*
*Pencil*
8 iridescent shades

*professional*
*Eyelash*
*Curler*

*Brow and Lash*
*Brush n' Comb*

*precision*
*Eyebrow*
*Tweezers*

# The first thing a lady puts on... Fragrance by Avon

AVON BEAUTY DUST ... applied with a luxurious lamb's wool puff to envelop you in fragrance. In beautiful refillable containers designed to complement each fragrance: Persian Wood, Here's My Heart and other Avon favorites.

AVON COLOGNE MISTS ... Sprayed on in a glorious selection of distinctive fragrances. The newest — and already beloved by millions — Topaze! In new dressing table bottles, Avon's Cologne Mists give lasting pleasure.

What a lovely way to start the day — with fascinating fragrance by Avon!

"AVON CALLING" at your home with the newest, the best in cosmetics and fragrances.

## AVON cosmetics
RADIO CITY, NEW YORK

AVON COSMETICS FOR ALL THE FAMILY ARE BROUGHT TO YOUR HOME BY YOUR AVON REPRESENTATIVE

## What makes this compact different?

rst: it holds the one and only shade of pressed face powder made to order just for you! Second: our ained consultant creates it right before your eyes, hand-blending to match, correct and enhance our coloring. Third: there's just nothing like it in all the world. $2.50 plus x. At favored department and specialty stores, here and in Canada. *Charles of the Ritz*

*"But you've just got to see me, doctor. I woke up in the dead of night feeling practically middle-aged."*

FOSTER GRANT # 2504, $1.98

*"With 5,000 Brahmas up on the mesa and 30 hands down with the mumps, Mary Beth, I reckon I'll just have to pass up the Paris openings this spring."*

*"We all make mistakes, Mr. Bond. Now buckle up your trench coat and get out of here."*

## Isn't that Mia Farrow behind those Foster Grants?

MIA FARROW has become a name to conjure with. Our delicate task was to discover whether our Foster Grants could conjure with Mia, could play tricks with her celebrated psyche and bring out the hidden her. With a star so young, we couldn't be sure.

We needn't have worried. No sooner had she slipped behind her first pair than the metamorphosis began. You can see for yourself. That's the fun of sunglasses. We call it the Spell of the Shades.

Nobody's sure why, but that mysterious something that comes over people behind sunglasses is probably the reason so many people are wearing them today. People who've never been near a beach, who never come out 'til the sun goes down. That's why they've got wardrobes of them, where they used to own just a pair. That's why they're as popular in Hong Kong as they are in Hollywood.

What's more, millions of them are Foster Grants. Because we happen to be #1 in the business. Far and away.

Of course Mia doesn't care about that. She probably doesn't even care that Foster Grant ff77 lenses pass strict U.S. eye protection tests, while many of the fancy-priced imports fail.

Does she care that we make more styles, in more colors, in more sizes than anybody—from $1 to $5? We do, even if she doesn't.

So there.  ©FOSTER GRANT, LEOMINSTER, MASS.

FOSTER GRANT # 5002, $5.00

*"Incomparable I may be, Gregory, but you can't seriously expect me to play a love scene opposite that."*

FOSTER GRANT # 3108 $2.98

*"Frankly, mother, I'd be a lot happier if you didn't even try to Watusi."*

# Keep-easy hair by
## *Kanekalon*®

Kanekalon's miracle wigs, falls, wiglets, curls take the care out of hair . . . let you pick up and go-go at a minute's notice.
No upkeep. No setting. Wash them out in a second, give them a whisk with

a comb, and they're ready for anything. Even wind and rain. Wear them now, or stuff them in your handbag for later.
They're made of Kanekalon modacrylic fibers—so natural, so lustrous, so for-real

they even fool experts. Match or mix every popular shade, even those wanted Frosts. Available at fine stores everywhere. Just be sure you find Kanekalon on the label.

Nothing like Kanekalon hair for instant beauty.
**Kanekalon**®
Osaka, Japan

**Every Girl is a Queen in her** *Nadine*

FORMALS AND PARTY DRESSES

# L'Aiglon

## What ever became of the little black dress?

If girls are wearing white this year, credit Acrilan.® It makes possible the first washable white dresses that look glamour-ous! They're designed by L'Aiglon in Heller's double-knit of <u>100% Acrilan acrylic fiber</u>. Also, scarlet, amber, soft green and—for those who can't live without it—a classic knock-out black. Dresses: left 8-18, right 10-20. Each, about $23. Chemstrand, New York 1, a Division of Monsanto Chemical Company, makes Acrilan acrylic fiber. Fashions by **L'Aiglon.**

**A**
ACRILAN
acrylic fiber
CHEMSTRAND

# for the many faces of

## You are Eve...

the eternal woman, with a hundred faces to beguile and fascinate
Which face do you wear this hour, Eve? Remember, your eyes hold the
secret of your every mood! Look into your mirror... are those the
deepening, gleaming eyes of your Siren face? Will a raised brow
announce the haughty Queen? Or will those silky lashes turn shyly
down, inviting tenderness? Your eyes speak for you, Eve... so make
the most of their subtle beauty.... always!.... with Maybelline.

For exquisitely expressive brows, Maybelline Self-Sharpener Eyebrow
Pencil... for eyes that deepen and glow, Maybelline Iridescent Eye
Shadow... a touch of scintillation with Maybelline Fluid Eye Liner
then lashes transformed, curled, colored and separated with the
exciting Maybelline achievement, Magic Mascara
with self-contained Spiral Brush.

Let Maybelline, the most prized eye cosmetics in the world,
reveal all the hidden beauty of your eyes.

# Maybelline
### devoted exclusively to eye beauty

Maybelline Magic Mascara Fluid Eye Liner Iridescent Eye Shadow Stick Self-Sharpener Eyebrow Pencil, $1 each

*Maybelline, 1961*

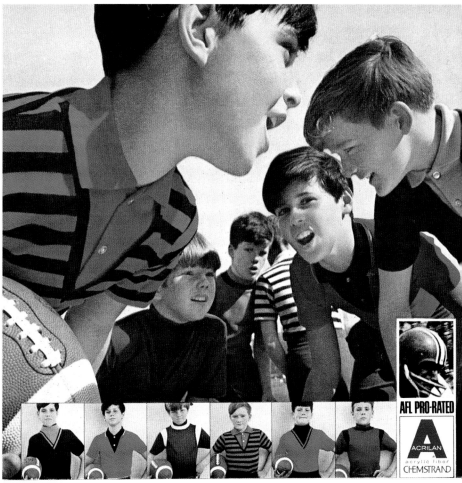

# All-Star Material

100% Acrilan® acrylic knits are great for rugged play
because we made them that way. They wear and wear,
keep their original shape, their true colors. Completely
machine washable. And boys like the big-league looks
of these Towncraft shirts—they're Pro-Rated™. At 1700
J. C. Penney stores, coast to coast. Sizes 6 to 18 **2.49**

**ALWAYS FIRST QUALITY**

*Penneys, 1966*

# COLLECTORS' ITEMS:
## RACY CARDIGANS IN
# BOY-PROOF ACRILAN®

Boys really go for these handsome he-man cardigans with their beefy knit beauty, their razzle-dazzle colors. Mothers love the way they hold their shape, their size, their vibrant colors—through almost endless machine-washings. Count on Penney's to see that extra value is knit into every stitch, from their rich brushed texture to their ample cut. Get these color-rich cardigans for your young collectors—in Hot Rod Red with two-tone grey panels, or Model-T Black with white/grey panels. Sizes 6 to 20. At most of J. C. Penney Company's 1700 stores, coast to coast—charge it! A Penney's exclusive at **6.95**

# The most beautiful western boots ever created!

## Golden ANGUS
### ACME BOOTS

A magnificent "Steerhead" design . . . richly inlaid with golden leathers! Intricate multi-color stitching! Eye-catching underlays! The Golden Angus is Acme's finest . . . the most beautiful of all western boots—ever! Many colors and combinations! Many styles of heels and toes! Your Acme dealer will be glad to show you!

Design patent applied for.

Mens Style No. 4850

Boys and Girls Style No. 2213

Boys and Girls Style No. 2209

## WORLD'S LARGEST BOOTMAKERS

### They cost less than you think!

Mens . . . . . . . . . . . . . . from $16.95
Boys and Girls . . . . . from $5.95 - $10.95, according to size

Acme Boots are worn by stars and featured players of Warner Bros. western television and motion picture productions.

Clint Walker stars in "CHEYENNE"

Will Hutchins stars in "SUGARFOOT"

Jack Kelly and James Garner star in "MAVERICK"

Boys and Girls Style No. 2760

Boys and Girls Style No. 2722

Boys and Girls Style No. 2743

Ask your dealer for an Acme Gift Certificate!

Acme Boot Company, Inc., Clarksville, Tennessee

A SUBSIDIARY OF PHILADELPHIA AND READING CORPORATION

**Here's**
# TOP QUALITY and AUTHENTIC STYLE

**"FAWN"**
4" brim; Herring-bone Weave; Fawn Color......$5.00

# GRAND ENTRY® WESTERN *Straws*

## SEE THESE SMART STYLES AT YOUR FAVORITE STORE NOW

Make a "grand entry" every time with one of these handsome, authentic western straws. Both feature leather ventilated sweatband with moisture-resistant liner, ventilated crown and enclosed brim wire for easy, permanent shaping. They're soil-resistant, too.

You'll be proud of the good looks and pleased with the top quality workmanship of either style.

**"DESERT SAND"**
3½" brim; Pearly Finish; Desert Sand Color......$5.00

**If not available, write your nearest distributor for the name of the dealer who handles this quality line of GRAND ENTRY HATS**

**GRAND ENTRY HAT CO. • 2625 Sidney Street • St. Louis 4, Mo.**

*Grand Entry Hat Co., 1960*

▶ *Burlington, 1962*

**National Velvet Headbands** Burlington's racy young fashion idea worn by Lori Martin and Carole Wells, stars of MGM's "National Velvet," on NBC-TV. Keeps your hair divinely smooth...on a galloping horse, in a dashing convertible, dancing, romancing, or whatever. Imported Bur-Mil stretch velvet, excitingly textured; 12 colors, vivacious, flirtatious, outrageously flattering. Only 89c in variety stores. One size fits every filly.

# winner in the st-r-e-t-c-h

BURLINGTON RIBBON MILLS, 505 Fifth Ave. N.Y. 16 a division of Burlington Industries

Burlington
QUALITY

# I dreamed I was

# WANTED
## in my Maidenform* bra

**'FRAME-UP'\* new bra with 3-way support**
Embroidered panels frame, outline and separate the cups. Extra-firm supports at the sides give you extra uplift. Stretch band at the bottom keeps the bra snug and securely in place. It's a 'Frame-up'—in A, B, C cups.

IT'S A STEAL, AT
**$1⁵⁹**

*REG. U. S. PAT. OFF. ©1963 BY MAIDENFORM, INC., MAKERS OF BRAS, GIRDLES, SWIMSUITS

# I dreamed
## barged down the Nile in my *maidenform* bra

Jarman, 1965        ▶ Etonic, 1969

# SHARK!

**ETONIC®**

A —'Merican Sportcoat—trim-cut—$22.95.
Happy American Tipper Knit Shirt—$ 5.00.
Happy American Sheen Frat Bermudas—$ 5.00.

B —'Merican Authentic Down Sportshirt—$5.95.
C —'Merican Islander Shorts — side-tab—$5.95.
Earl-Glo® linings Sani-tized® treated for hygienic freshness.

# MAKE PAPPY HAPPY with a fit-for-a-rajah gift

of the coolest sportswear west of the Himalayas! Fresh,
authentic colors and patterns are translated into breezy
cottons for Father's Day by

**FATHER'S DAY IS JUNE 19.**

Also boy-sized, boy-priced. Made in Canada, too. McGregor-Doniger Inc., New York 19, N.Y.

*McGregor, 1960*

**Celaperm***

# Who is he?

He's a happy beachcomber in
Brentwood sportswear that
Celaperm keeps color-bright

Lucky Dad, they gave him the perfect plaid for summertime sunning. And, thanks to Celaperm, those colors are sealed-in to stay. Here's a comfortable fabric whose durability is matched only by its good looks.

Brentwood's matching sets in Celaperm acetate and cotton novelty plaid by Nashcombe. Walking shorts, about $5; sizes 30-42. Jacket, about $7; sizes S, M, L. Beachcomber pants, about $6; matching knit shirt, about $4. In red, blue, brown, or black plaids. Available at fine stores everywhere. For stores carrying "Who is he?" sportswear, see opposite page.

Celanese® Celaperm®

Celaperm...a *Celanese* contemporary fiber

Celanese, 1960

## you're a NaTuraL WoNder

## in natural-look h·i·s piper 61 slacks

Get a look-see at yourself in these new clean-cut Pipers and you'll lay your moola on the line for a few pair fast! They fit like wallpaper on the wall, ride down low on your hips, cuffs are out and belts are nowhere (extension waistband with hidden side tabs handle the up-keep). Try 'em, man!

*Washable Cotton or Dacron and Cotton in Nailchecks, Cords, Twills, Sateens, Plaids, District Checks. $4.95 to $8.95*

**h·i·s**
SPORTSWEAR ®
Don't envy H·I·S...wear them

At wonder-full stores . . . or write
h·i·s sportswear
230 Fifth Avenue, New York 1, N. Y.

Another natural wonder...Grand Geyser,
Yellowstone National Park, Wyoming.

ZIPPER BY TALON

*H.I.S. Sportswear, 1961* ▸ *OshKosh Sportswear, 1960*

SMART
MEN WITH
MONEY —
FASHION-ALERT
MONEY —
HAVE ZEROED
THEIR FASHION
FOCUS ON
OSHKOSH SPORTSWEAR.
THEY SCREAM
FOR MORE
OF THESE
GUARANTEED
BEST/PREST SLACKS
AND JEANS.
DO YOU
WANT TO BE
OUT OF FOCUS —
AND OUT
OF FASHION?

**FASHION FOCUS**

**OSHKOSH**
*Sportswear*

STRIDE • DUDES • TITUS • STANCE • ALL BEST/PREST

# There are some men a hat won't help

If you look anything like the fellow in the picture, you can stop reading right now. Wearing a hat won't do a thing for you.

No miracles happen when you put on a hat, but it can make the rough, competitive road between you and the top a little easier to travel.

You look more of a man with a hat on, and the men who run things have a deeply ingrained executive habit of reserving responsible jobs for those young men who look mature enough to handle them.

They may be right, or they may be wrong, but there's no denying that they're in charge. So it pays to humor them. Most business executives we've talked to prefer to hire men who wear hats.

We don't imply that going bareheaded marks you for failure. In the long run, it's what's under the hat that counts. Wearing a hat is just one of those little things that make it easier for a young man to get to where he wants to go. *You say you're in a hurry? Where's your hat?*

*A little friendly advice to young men in a hurry, published in the selfish interests of the hat industry by the Hat Corporation of America, 530 Fifth Avenue, New York 36, New York.*

*Knox, 1962* ◄

*Hat Corporation of America, 1961*

# New from London:

bold-striped...

English broadcloth...

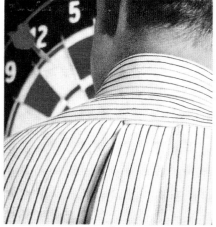

now in Gant...

button-downs

*Regent Stripe—luxuriant English broadcloth with a silken facade; its evocative stripes on eggshell ground speak for themselves. Worn with tweeds or worsteds, this Gant Regent Stripe shirt has élan in a gentlemanly manner. In a varied choice of multicolored stripes. About $9 at discerning stores. For one nearest you, write Gant Shirtmakers, New Haven, Connecticut.*

GANT
SHIRTMAKERS

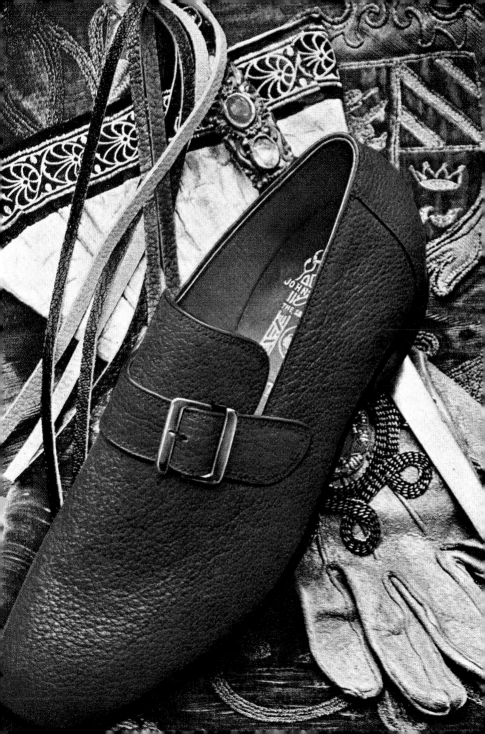

THE CATALINA® MAN *discovers* Creslan
ACRYLIC FIBE

For the golfer who takes his sports and sportshirts seriously, this handso
lightweight shirt is knit to fit in 70% Creslan acrylic fiber, 30% nylon. It le
a man swing with comfort. It dries into perfect shape after launderir
In sporting colors, about $12.95. Cyanamid makes the Creslan acry
fiber; Catalina makes the garments. American Cyanamid Company, New Yo

Color co-ordinated hosiery available from Esquire So

CYANAMID

FATHER'S DAY • JUNE 19

choose the gift
that comes through
with flying colors...

*Old Spice*

for Dad

(above) After Shave Lotion, Stick Deodorant, Cologne, Body Talcum, Shampoo, 5.00

### (*A little reminder*)

This is an elephant. Wearing a pair of pants.

The elephant is loxodonta africana. The pants are "Sanforized-Plus". The elephant is wrinkled. It's not his fault. He was made that way. The pants are never wrinkled. They were made that way, too.

They were made to be labeled, "Sanforized-Plus". Repeat. "Sanforized-Plus". The tag that lets you trust in wash-and-wear. Just as "Sanforized" protects you against shrinkage in cottons, so "Sanforized-Plus"

assures you of wash-and-wear that really works. There's no more "wash-and-wonder." If you see it is marked "Sanforized-Plus", you can be sure:

It won't wrinkle from washing. It'll stay smooth while worn. It'll survive wash after wash. It won't shrink out of fit.

In other words, "Sanforized-Plus" means wash-and-wear that really works. So always be sure to look for our label. Our model never forgets. Don't you!

**·SANFORIZED·**
TRADE MARK
**says it won't shrink out of fit**

**·SANFORIZED plus·**
TRADEMARK
**says it's tested wash-and-wear**

CLUETT, PEABODY & CO., INC., PERMITS USE OF ITS TRADEMARK "SANFORIZED-PLUS" ONLY ON FABRICS WHICH MEET ITS ESTABLISHED TEST REQUIREMENTS FOR SHRINKAGE, SMOOTHNESS AFTER WASHING, CREASE RECOVERY, TENSILE STRENGTH AND TEAR STRENGTH. FABRICS BEARING THE TRADEMARK "SANFORIZED" OR "SANFORIZED-PLUS" WILL NOT SHRINK MORE THAN 1% BY THE GOVERNMENT'S STANDARD TEST.

*Sanforized, 1963*

Beatniks are against all garments labeled "Sanforized" or "Sanforized-Plus".

Naturally.

These two labels destroy their whole image. You can't look "beat" and neat at the same time.

"Sanforized" stops *shrinkage*—an old beatnik stand-by for appalling appearance.

"Sanforized-Plus" fights *wrinkles* as well...and also assures long-lasting fabric.

So, even after days of exposure to rain and folk music in the park, clothes with our labels hold stubbornly to their original size and smoothness.

If you *like* looking like a wayward accordion, avoid "Sanforized" and "Sanforized-Plus".

Otherwise, always be sure you see our trademarks before you buy. It's not hard. They're everywhere.

·SANFORIZED·
TRADE & MARK
**says it won't shrink out of fit**

·SANFORIZED **plus**·
TRADEMARK
**says it's tested wash-and-wear**

*Sanforized, 1963*

# Hi-fi fan Ernie Klack

## finds Carter's <u>knitted</u> boxer shorts an indispensable component

For harmony in the Klack household, Ernie traditionally turns to the classic — *knitted* boxer shorts by Carter's. His good wife, Irma, is happy: she knows these *cotton knits* reject any discordant need for ironing. Ernie is happy: he's shamelessly flattered by their trim styling, outrageously pampered by their soft comfort. Now the secret is out and you can be happy, too. Just keep in mind that the boxers are *knit* and the name is *Carter's*.

*Ernie Klack is any guy who wears Carter's knitted boxer shorts and considers it uncivilized (and uncomfortable) to wear any other kind.*

# *Carter's*
### THE WILLIAM CARTER CO. NEEDHAM HEIGHTS. MASS.

**MEANS COMFORT IN KNITTED BOXER SHORTS ... BRIEFS ... T-SHIRTS ... ATHLETIC SHIRTS**

**FOULARD PRINT Knit Boxers, $1.75 ... at these and other fine stores:** ATLANTA, Rich's • BOSTON, Jordan Marsh Co. • CHICAGO, Baskin — All Stores CINCINNATI, John Shillito Co. • DALLAS, Jas. K. Wilson • DAYTON, The Metropolitan Co. • DENVER, COLORADO SPRINGS, May D & F • FLINT, A. M. Davison Co. • HARRISBURG, Pomeroy's LOS ANGELES, Bullock's—Downtown, Westwood, Pasadena, Santa Ana • LONG BEACH & SANTA ANA, Buffum's • MINNEAPOLIS, Dayton's • NEW YORK, B. Altman & Co., Wallachs, Franklin Simon • NEWARK, Hahne & Co. • ORLANDO, Rutland's • PHOENIX, Diamonds • ST. LOUIS, Wolff's • SALT LAKE CITY, Z.C.M.I. • SEATTLE-TACOMA, Klopfensteins • WILMINGTON, Kennard's

# The new button-down guarantee.

*Chemstrand, 1964*

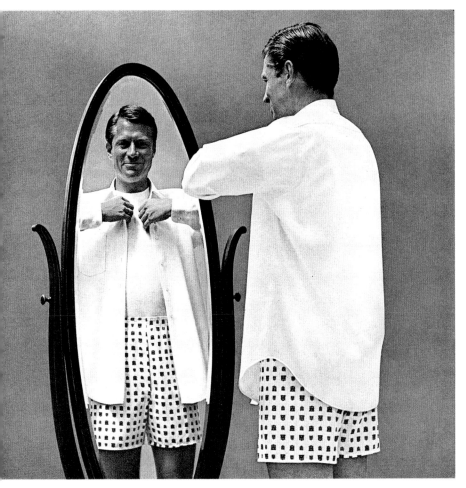

# ven if he's taking you on a holiday vacation here's no need to pay a fancy price for his underwear and shirts... not if they're Fruit of the Loom.

When a man dresses up for something special, e wants to feel special. You can give him hat feeling for a lot less than you think. or just 89¢ you can get him long-wearing ruit of the Loom Sanforized® wash-and-wear otton shorts. With extra seat room, extra eg room, extra give and take in the waist. Even ew Golden Fruit of the Loom underwear s just $1.15. And it's permanent press Dacron®

polyester and cotton. Same savings go for Fruit of the Loom permanent press shirts. Trim, tapered, fine quality dress and sport shirts, from only $2.99. See, there's no need to pay a fancy price for his underwear and shirts. Not if they're Fruit of the Loom. Get him some for Christmas. *The price is so low, the value so high... you can't afford not to buy Fruit of the Loom.*

A subsidiary of Northwest Industries Inc.
Fruit of the Loom, 1290 Avenue of the Americas, New York, N.Y. 10019

*DuPont's reg. T.M.

en's Underwear—69¢, 89¢ & $1.15/Men's Shirts—from $2.99/Boys' Underwear—49¢ to 89¢/Infants' Underwear—49¢ to 99¢

▶ *Fruit of the Loom, 1968*

# polka dots' place is not on your face

Gloves, gowns—even galoshes—are perfect in polka dots. But complexions—uh-uh. Now, Tussy Medicare has the problem skin well in hand. It hides and helps heal blackheads, pimples,—even acne—quickly, comfortably . . . gives your skin a clear lovely look in just three simple steps.

**TRIPLE ACTION TREATMENT**

**1** To deep-cleanse skin, to remove pore-clogging oil and infection-causing bacteria, and keep them away —Tussy Medicated Creamy Masque. Smoothing, soothing!

**2** To stimulate circulation locally, to help float away impurities—Tussy Medicated Skin Toner. Wonderfully cool and refreshing!

**3** To make blemishes vanish from view—Tussy Medicated Lotion. Helps dry up excess oil, soften a coarsened skin. A true face saver!

Tussy Medicare Triple-Action Treatment, $2.95
Tussy Medicare items, each $1
Tussy Medicated Touch-Up Stick for quick cover-ups, $1
*all prices plus tax*

© 1960 TUSSY, 635 PARK AVENUE, NEW YORK

TUSSY *cares for you*

# Be cagey about crow's feet

## try TUSSY EYE CREAM

Did you know that almost everyone has very delicate, dry skin around the eyes? That's why Tussy Eye Cream was made. It is a special blend of active oils to pamper that sensitive area. Smooth it all around your eyes to help shoo away crow's feet, to help ward off tired lines. Use it faithfully every night and soon you won't believe your pretty eyes! Just $1.00 and $1.75, *plus tax*

Queen Size

to do a delicate job quickly

Elégance
Lady Sunbeam

Elégance
Lady Sunbeam
ELECTRIC SHAVER

The gentlest, yet the fastest way to be sure

Sunbeam, 1960

**In this**     **push-button age...**

Just push the button. Instantly, myriad sparklets of mist diffuse to the warmth of your skin. As they envelop you in fragrance, you move in a magnetic aura he can't resist. The fragrance? Yours to command. For Prince Matchabelli brings you a new presentation of Cologne Spray Mist in not just one, but four fragrances...Abano, Stradivari, Beloved, or Wind Song...all on push-button control.

*Prince Matchabelli, 1960*

Crown your hair with the shining secret
...the golden egg-enriched shampoo.
From Helene Curtis.

*Helene Curtis, 1961*

# AT LAST!
# A NO-MESS,
# NO-DRIP WAY
# TO COLOR
# YOUR HAIR!

# color foam by

## Du Barry

Now add color to your
hair with "push-button"
ease. *Pffffft....*it even comes out foam.

With your eyes wide open, now sit in front of your mirror and, with the same
ease you change your makeup, bring exciting new beauty and shimmering
highlights to your hair. You'll blend in gray with new perfection, too—all with
the push of a button. No mess . . . no drip . . . no run.

COLOR FOAM goes on in minutes, stays on for shampoo after shampoo.
Ten flattering colors to choose from. All leave your hair looking and
feeling soft, natural, and delightfully manageable. For that beautiful
bright new look your hairdresser knows so well . . . use COLOR FOAM.

© 1963 DuBarry

*Du Barry, 1963*

WOOL

All aglow in natural wool that drinks up color . . . a luxurious mohair and wool cardigan with an air-lightness that brightens the day and a rich softness that lightens the night. The wool flannel skirt is color-matched and tailored to perfection. Ragtime Orange, Flapper Blue, White or pastels. Sweater, about $14. Longer version, about $16. Sizes 34 to 40. Skirt, about $10. Sizes 8 to 16, 7 to 15. At fine stores everywhere.

IRWILL KNITWEAR CORP., 1407 BROADWAY, NEW YORK

DESIGNED TO BE LIVED IN

JANE IRWILL

JANE IRWILL RECOMMENDS CKC COLD WATER WASH

SPONSORED JOINTLY WITH AMERICAN WOOL COUNCIL

*There is nothing **newer** in fashion than Natural Wool Loomed and Knitted in America.*

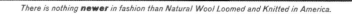

*Jane Irwill, 1961* ▶ *Davidow, 1966* ▶▶ *The Formfit Company, 1962*

LONDON    PARIS

DAVIDOW

NEW YORK

*the label to ask for*

# Luxury trimming...Lycra with Paisley Pastel for

## *that* Formfit *feeling!*

Luxury trimming . . . luxury slimming. Both yours in this new Formfit Long-Leg Skippies. Lycra spandex molds superbly with a firm light touch you barely feel. Delicate paisley panels of nylon sheer over tricot. Soft neutral toffee-toned print over exquisite pastels like this Sparkling Champagne. Also in White, Ariel Blue and Petal Pink.

*Formfit Skippies Long-Leg Style 781.* Lycra* spandex with nylon tricot front and side panels; satin elastic back panel. (Nylon, acetate, spandex, cotton.) S. M. L. *(Regular length pantie or girdle $8.95)* $10⁹⁵

*Matching Formfit Laughter Bra Style 480.* 32A-38C. $3⁹⁵

THE FORMFIT COMPANY
A FASHION DIVISION OF GENESCO
CHICAGO • NEW YORK • TORONTO • PARIS • LONDON • SYDNEY
*DU PONT TRADEMARK

For The Bath.

CHANEL

Eau de Cologne from 3.50, Oil For The Bath from 5.00, After-Bath Oil Spray 5.00, Bath Powder 5.00.

**Réplique
will not turn you into
a sultry, sexy
siren.**

**It will not
transform you
into a
simple, unsullied ingénue.**

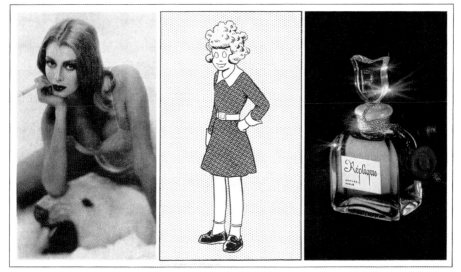

**Réplique
is for women
who are interesting
to begin with.**

# Does she... or doesn't she?*

## Hair color so natural only her hairdresser knows for sure!

**Though the look of beauty** is a changing thing, *she* knows the quality of freshness never loses its appeal. And her wholesome good looks are as much a matter of grooming and fresh, sparkling hair color as of pretty features. With Miss Clairol, it's easy to keep hair beautiful—silky, radiant with natural-looking color. These are the qualities that distinguish Miss Clairol from all other haircolorings.

**And this is why hairdressers** all over the world recommend Miss Clairol, use it every time to revitalize fading color. They know its *automatic color timing* is most dependable and Miss Clairol *really* covers gray. But most of all, they love the lively, natural look of it, the soft, ladylike tone. And so will you. So try Miss Clairol yourself. Today. Takes only minutes. Creme Formula or Regular.

CREME FORMULA

**MISS CLAIROL**

HAIR COLOR BATH

LIGHTENS AS IT COLORS
NATURAL-LOOKING COLOR
COVERS GRAY COMPLETELY

Guaranteed by
Good Housekeeping

REPLACEMENT OR REFUND OF MONEY
IF NOT AS ADVERTISED THEREIN

**MISS CLAIROL®** HAIR COLOR BATH* MORE WOMEN USE MISS CLAIROL THAN ALL OTHER HAIRCOLORING COMBINED

*TM ©1960 CLAIROL INCORPORATED, STAMFORD, CONN. AVAILABLE ALSO IN CANADA.

Drench your hair in luxury
with Liquid Prell...
*the extra-rich shampoo!*

Suit by Dalton of America

# Marked for greatness
### This superb suit with the mark of the world's best...pure wool

Excellence. In design, detail, tailoring. That's what you get when a designer *cares*. In fabric, you get the world's best. Pure wool. Wool that drapes gracefully, tailors beautifully. Wool with the natural resilience to keep in shape. Designers of distinction choose wool. They're proud to wear the mark, created

This mark was created by the Wool Bureau, Inc.
It is awarded to quality products made of the world's best pure wool.

by the Wool Bureau, given only to fashions made of the world's best pure wool. Look for the wool mark. Wherever you find it, you find devotion to excellence. Dalton selected pure wool in an exciting crochet knit to bring you this dazzling 3-piece suit. The Wool Bureau, Inc., 360 Lexington Ave., New York 17, N.Y.

# The LADY REMINGTON® Shaver could be too intimate to give her.

## So send it.

Once sent, go about your business.

Before you know it, she'll come to you, murmuring her gratitude. She'll have excellent reason. After all, it's the only Lady around that adjusts for legs and underarms.

Adjusts down, quick as a wink, legs not only feel beautiful, they look beautiful.

Adjusts up, even quicker, sensitive underarms are smoothed. So gentle, she can use a deodorant without any irritation.

This is the Lady with the on-off switch. Very handy. (Phone rings. Shaver off. No bother.)

The LADY REMINGTON. Dressed in its "Swing-Away" boudoir case. Very special. With three pastel colors to choose from: orchid, blue or gold. Pretty.

A closing thought: the LADY REMINGTON does cost a bit more. But, then, it's just the kind of gift she'd expect from her Santa.

Another lovely lady . . . the cordless LADY REMINGTON® LEKTRONIC. Has two separate heads, one for underarms, one for legs. Also works with a cord if she forgets to recharge.

*Lady Remington, 1964*

# you're all wet...

# but your hairdo isn't!

You're the belle of the beach! Sava-Wave inner rim in Kleinert's fashion swim caps "seals out" water, keeps your hair dry and beautiful. Ondine (shown) hugs head in a cascade of face-flattering petals. New ombré color effect in pink, green, blue, gold, black and orange.

Price $6. Other Sava-Wave caps from $1.25.

**Who would have thought of it but Kleinert's.**

485 FIFTH AVE., N. Y., N. Y. · TORONTO, CANADA · LONDON, ENGLAND

*Kleinert's*
SWIM CAPS

Amazing Quick Tanning Discovery by COPPERTONE®

# Tans you in 3 to 5 Hours Without the Sun

**INDOORS,**
tans you overnight

Apply Q.T. at bedtime (following directions). Wake up next morning with a gorgeous tan! Q.T. tans you *by a new principle.* Wonderful if you couldn't tan before or don't have time to sunbathe!

# or With the Sun

**OUTDOORS,**
deepens your tan

Apply Q.T. next day in the sun—and your tan becomes deeper, richer! Outdoors, Q.T. lets the sun tan inner skin layers, while screening out burning rays with Coppertone's own scientific sunscreen agent.

# Q.T. gives you a DOUBLE TAN !

**Tans parts of the body the sun can not reach, for the best all-over tan you can get—and the easiest and fastest! Gives best protection against sunburn, too!**

Now practically everybody can be smoothly, glamorously tanned . . . without the time and trouble tanning usually takes. What a boon for busy people! For all who burn easily or find it hard to tan! Q.T. by Coppertone was created to make tanning easy.

Q.T. contains Ketochromin—a natural tanning agent—that reacts with the protein in the outer layer of your skin to give you a smooth, glorious tan fast, and without sunlight. Then, helps the sun deepen your tan outdoors!

Safety Proved in Medical Tests—Q.T. is safe for every normal skin type; has been clinically tested by doctors, used by millions. Q.T. contains no dyes to streak or discolor skin.

Instead, its emollients and conditioners soften, moisturize, benefit your skin, as its sunscreen agent protects you against painful sunburn.

Authorities say it's dangerous to get a *suntan too fast.* So start your tan now with Q.T. in your own home. Then, outdoors, let Q.T. and the sun make your tan still deeper. Have a beautiful tan when you first put on play clothes—and stay tan all summer long!

*Glamorize Legs, Save on Stockings!* Q.T. "tan-grooms" legs, so smoothly, so evenly, there's no need for hot stockings. Use Q.T. to touch up pale body areas, too. End embarrassing "strap marks." Look better in your low-cut dresses, all year round.

In Tests—Surpassed Almost a FULL WEEK'S Normal Suntanning! In tests by a prominent skin specialist—overnight use of Q.T. gave a deeper tan than a full hour's exposure to sun daily for almost a week! Subjects used popular suntan lotion or cream (by other makers) on one side of backs—left other side covered for 6 days—then Q.T. was applied to untanned side. Next day the Q.T. tan outscored the 6-day outdoor suntans!

Men — Use Q.T. for a Vital-Looking Tan All Year! Don't look "pale as paste." And don't let your vacation tan fade. *Keep* it with Q.T.

**GUARANTEE:** Money back from Q.T. if you don't find Q.T. double tan the finest tan you've had. Start Q.T. now. Save on large size.

*Coppertone and Q.T. are quality products of Plough, Inc.*

Coppertone, 1965

Sunglasses are Spectaculars by Renauld—"Classic" Model

## Sea & Ski saves a lot of lifeguards

Ever notice the suntan lotion on the
lifeguard stands? Notice how often it's Sea & Ski!
It blocks out most burning rays—up to
47% more than its nearest competitor. Lets in up to 52%
more tanning rays! And Sea & Ski
moisturizers keep skin from getting dry and peely.
So stay out as long as you want with
Sea & Ski Suntan Lotion—one of 8 great suntanning
products perfected for Sea & Ski by
the Desert Research Institute.

## You sure will TAN
( sure won't burn )
## with SEA & SKI

**NEW OIL-LESS OIL!**
A Sea & Ski breakthrough! Gives
oil users the sleek, shiny tan they love
without the greasy mess of old-style oils.

**NEW SNOOTIE**
Invisible extra protection
for nose, lips and ears.

© 1964 Sea & Ski Co., Div. Botany Industries, Inc., Reno, N

*Sea & Ski, 1964*

have a love affair with the sun

wear nothing but Bain de Soleil

Bare and tawny you in a unique Bain de Soleil tiger-tan. What more could a girl wear? Choose rich dark in cream or fluid, or new non-oily white. $2.

*Bain de Soleil, 1966*

▶ *Max Factor, 1960*

for Christmas...

he MALE FACTOR     a new ingredient in men's
toiletries that separates the men from the boys...
but not the girls...by **MAX FACTOR**

TRIMLEE

UPTIGHTLEE

HIPLEE

NEATLEE

*Lee Jeans, 1968*

# h.i.s stripe types

## (Which type are you?)

**Boat Neck.** You're modest about your muscles so you cover most of them.

**Tank Top.** You're proud of your muscles so you show 'em.

**Muscle Shirt.** You think you have muscles

**Crew Neck.** You just like stripes.

**V-Neck.** You think plunging necklines look good on you as well as on the birds.

**Stripe of a different type.** This one you don't wear. You watch. And she'll return the glances, whichever model you wear. They're cotton knits, each in 8 colors. $4 and $5. h.i.s, 16 E. 34th St., N.Y. 10016

*H.I.S. Sportswear, 1964*

**Who's the wild strummer?**

Maybro's hipsters know the carefree score with Fortrel. Machine
wash, need only touch-up ironing. Crown's fabrics of Fortrel
polyester, rayon and flax.
Ribbed knit top about $7.
hickory / tan / turquoise. Linen-like
pants in hickory, about $9. Both
-13. At Macy's New York;
The Broadway, So. California;
Macy's No. California;
John Wanamaker, Philadelphia;
Woodward & Lothrop,
Washington, D.C.

**Who sets the pace?**

Collegetown's duo sets the no-
iron pace in Fortrel with perma-
nent press. Not a wrinkle
after machine washing. Dan-
Press yarn dyed plaid of Fortrel
polyester and cotton and poplin of
Fortrel polyester and Avril rayon. Ber-
mudas, about $7. Midriff top, about $5.
Burgundy or navy. 5-15. At Stern
Brothers, New York; Forbes
& Wallace, Springfield;
D. H. Holmes Co., Ltd.,
New Orleans;
Miller's, Knoxville;
John Wanamaker,
Philadelphia.

# The Celanese Crowd-Pleasers...

Do the skate:

Skate right, clap hands.

Skate left.

Shake shoulders, roll hands.

Skaters position, lean forward.

Skate forward right, then left.

# Cut loose in Career Club™ Shirts

Career Club tapered shirts in cotton broadcloth with new hi-boy roll collar. 15 hot and sweet colors. $4. Slightly higher in the West. Get free dance booklet at your Career Club dealer. Or write to Dance, Truval Shirt Co. Inc., 350 Fifth Ave., N.Y.

*Career Club, 1967*

Do the boogaloo

Cut loose in
Career Club™ Shirts

*Career Club, 1967*

*Bondex, 1961*

USE DAILY: Unscrew cap at base and roll deodorant on underarm. Keep tightly capped when not in use

FRESH checks perspiration and instantly stops under-arm odor. Safe for fabrics and normal skin. Do not use

**Fresh** ®
ROLL-ON
DEODORANT

upsi daisy

Fresh Roll-on comes in an upside-down bottle
('cause it's the best way to give you the most effective roll-on deodorant!)

—the effectiveness of a cream with the convenience of on! Marvelous, upside-down Fresh is always creamy, drips…always flowing, never sticks…always gen-

tle, never fails. You stay fresh hour after busy hour with Fresh Roll-on…the deodorant that's an anti-perspirant, too. It's the one and only roll-on in the upside-down bottle!

*there's **nothing** fresher than* Fresh

Fresh, 1960

Part of the art of eve... *Catalina*

Shy violets not shy enough to seek cover

pop up in a *Jantzen* Bashful Bikini.

Who wouldn't smile upon nature at its best?

Even more glamorous when wet 15.95.
T.M.

# just wear a smile and a jantzen

Jantzen Inc., Portland 8, Oregon

# PINK
# IS FOR GIRLS

That's why Lustre-Creme is pink. Because it's made just
for girls. If you don't believe it, just breathe in
Lustre-Creme's pink fragrance. See. It's a little
too delicate for anyone *but* a girl! Now shampoo
with pink Lustre-Creme and feel how truly soft your hair
can be. So soft, it says "touch me." And he will!
Pink, creamy Lustre-Creme. It's the one shampoo
made just for girls. Because pink is just for girls.
You're a girl, aren't you?

You might be tickled pink to know that
Lustre-Creme is safe for color-treated hair.

*Lustre Creme, 1969*

▶ Lustre Creme, 19◉

# PINK IS FOR GIRLS

That's why girls like Lustre-Creme. It's the only pink shampoo.

Pink says we're rich, so rich your whole head becomes one great swirl of whipped-cream lather.

Pink says we leave hair soft, and inviting to touch.

And should a certain someone get too close, he'll notice that we have a delightful "pink" fragrance, too.

Pink, creamy Lustre-Creme. It's the one shampoo made just for girls. Because pink is just for girls.

You're a girl, aren't you?

Lustre
Creme.

LOTION
SHAMPOO

I dreamed I drove them wild
in my *maidenform* bra

What's black
and white
and red
all over?

**COMPLEXION: BRONZE**
COTY SUNSET ORANGE—a find for your lips, a flip for fingertips with costumes of orange rind. A fascinating light with azalea, biscuit and white.

**COMPLEXION: BRONZE**
COTY MAGNET RED—fabulous fillip with filbert brown fashions... raving beauty with navy... perfect partner with parrot green... gay with gray.

**COMPLEXION: BRONZE**
COTY PRECIOUS PINK—a rich, ripe sheen when you're in almond green ...a new sensation with mauve, peony and Spanish gold creations.

**COMPLEXION: PINK**
COTY CARDINAL RED—beautiful to behold with Spanish gold... subtly but surely steals the scene with scarlets, blues and almond green.

**COMPLEXION: PINK**
COTY FLAMINGO PINK—the bloom for lips and fingertips with azalea costumes... fashion's favorite with pale blue, peony and biscuit beige.

**COMPLEXION: PINK**
COTY FLAME RED—the shimmer for you wearing new Bristol blue...glamour point of view with parrot green, white and hues of butternut beige.

**COMPLEXION: FAIR**
COTY MEDIUM—a taste sensation with biscuit creations... a flirt with filbert brown... downright dazzling with azalea and Bristol blue fashions.

**COMPLEXION: FAIR**
COTY ROSE—charming exclamation point with mauve... sweet elation with Spanish gold, enchanting sheen with aquamarine and almond green.

**COMPLEXION: FAIR**
COTY CARDINAL RED—matchmate for lips and fingertips with scarlet fashions...a happy hue with biscuit, almond green and new Bristol blue.

**COMPLEXION: ALABASTER**
COTY PICARDY PEACH—a peach with parrot green... divine with orange rind ... fashionable and fun with azalea and lemon ensembles.

**COMPLEXION: ALABASTER**
COTY MEDIUM—ultrafabulous with peony fashions (match your fingertips, too)... bright fascination with parrot green, aquamarine and white.

**COMPLEXION: ALABASTER**
COTY BRIGHT—beautiful light with pale blue fabrics...a treasure-trove with oatmeal and mauve ...a wonderful way with costumes of gray.

## SPRING FASHION FORECAST

Here's how to blend your lipstick and nail polish shades with your complexion and the newest spring fashions!

# HARMONY IN COLOR
### BY COTY

in vibrant, long-lasting Coty '24' lipstick and matching Super Sheen Nail Polish

Now the matching of colors is no longer a problem at all. Coty's new Harmony in Color does it for you! Here's all you do: First, find your complexion under each picture. Next, choose your favorite Coty lipstick color and matching nail polish. Finally, see your most complimentary costume color for spring, harmonized to you, color-blended by fashion experts and Coty. Look for Harmony in Color at your favorite Coty counter... today!

Look for this special Harmony in Color offer!

VIBRANT, LONG-LASTING COTY '24' LIPSTICK AND MATCHING SUPER SHEEN NAIL POLISH

REGULAR $2.00 VALUE
ONLY $1.50
REFILLS $1.
ALL PRICES PLUS TAX

No printed page can reproduce exactly the truly beautiful colors of Coty lipstick and nail polish. The colors shown here are even more beautiful on your lips and nails.

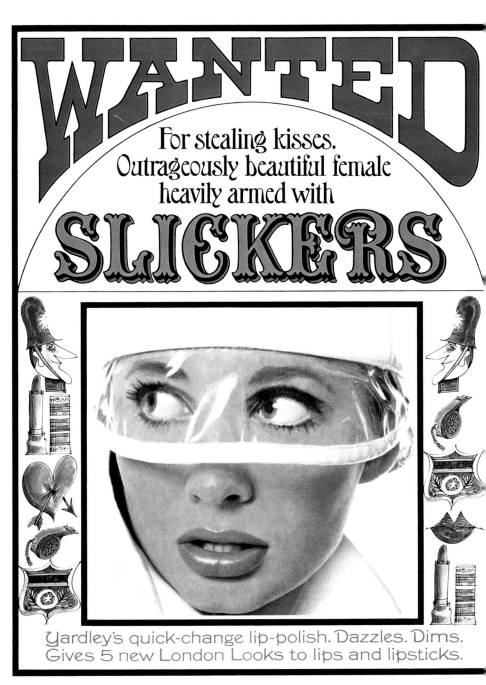

# WANTED

For stealing kisses.
Outrageously beautiful female
heavily armed with

# SLICKERS

Yardley's quick-change lip-polish. Dazzles. Dims.
Gives 5 new London Looks to lips and lipsticks.

*Yardley of London, 1966*

Cosmetic couture: creating custom-blended face powder to your beauty measurements. Boxed loose, $2 and $3. Pressed in a handsome compact, $2, plus tax. At our beauty bars in your favored department and specialty stores.

AZA 8, A WILD YOUNG UNDER-WHIMSY, IS HAPPENING.
SHOULD HAPPEN TO YOU.)

ND-DAFFY. SHEER NYLON WAFER-DOT BRA. PADDED, $5.00. UNPADDED, $4.25. MATCHING PANTIE GIRDLE; WHITE WITH YELLOW, GREEN AND PINK DOTS. $7.00
HE NEW PLAZA 8 COLLECTION BY PERMA-LIFT.

# Peter Pan
## invented a new kind of transistor.

## It turns <u>you</u> on.

The first girdle that doesn't look like one. Transistor®. Light and colorful. The smoothest, brightest shaper on the young scene. Just a wee circle of colorful **Caprolan®** and spandex powernet, knit in a new way to eliminate body seams. Try one and you'll have to have them all. They really turn you on—in blue, green, apricot or charcoal.

Fashion length panty girdle, S-M-L, $7. Short leg panty girdle, S-M-L, $6. Matching Transistor® bra with famous Fiber-Foam®. Average cup, 32 to 36, $5.

# Transistor®
# by Peter Pan

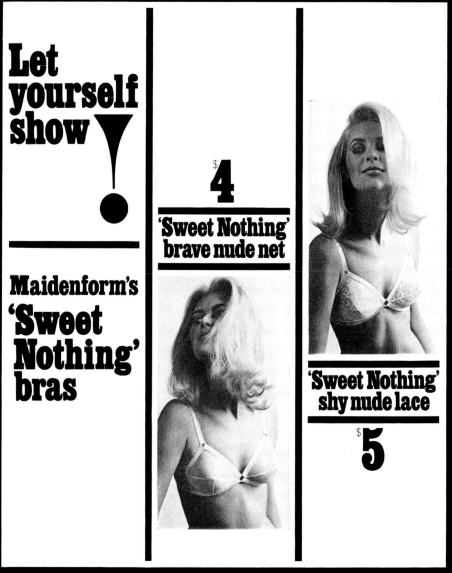

Let
yourself
show !

Maidenform's
'Sweet
Nothing'
bras

$4
'Sweet Nothing'
brave nude net

'Sweet Nothing'
shy nude lace
$5

# JUST FOR KICKS

## ORLON®

Legs, that's where the action is in Orlon* acrylic. And it all starts where a short skirt stops. Take your pick of the fun going on, this fall—patterns, textures, colors. All yum, all swinging in "Orlon". Try them. Just for kicks!

*DU PONT'S REGISTERED TRADEMARK. DU PONT MAKES FIBERS, NOT THE FASHIONS OR STOCKINGS SHOWN.

Better Things for Better Living . . . *through Chemistry*

Du Pont, 1966

Wrangler, 1966

# it's a contest...it's a snap with

Let your imagination play! Set the scene with a boy and a beach, you and a sunny day. Arrange the props to tell a story. Have a friend snap it up; send the photo to RMR Juniors. First and second prizes each month: a General Electric color television set, a General Electric "Century" portable TV set!

Pick up your official entry blank in your favorite swimsuit department. For the name of the one nearest you, write: Rose Marie Reid, Dept. 17-C, Van Nuys, Calif. NOTE: focus for flattery on a next-to-nothing waistline in GAIETY, fresh-cut elasticized sheath nipped by a cummerbund, in sizes 9-15, 19.95.

## RMR

ROSE MARIE REID

# juniors

*Rose Marie Reid, 1962*

**t is much better to give. That is why Jantzen swimtrunks are made of Chemstrand sharkskin.**

The most popular swimsuit in history has always been absolutely perfect, so we thought, but now Chemstrand Blue C Spandex
has come along to give something to perfection. Elasticized stretch sharkskin! This splendid blend, exactly right for stretch swimtrunks, is 78% acetate, 16% cotton, and 6% Chemstrand Blue C Spandex. As Frank Gifford, in the $7 webbed belt style, says, it
gives more than it gets. Jerry West wears crossed belt loop stretch, about $8. Bobby Hull is in the button tab stretch, about $6.
Comfortable, tough, good-looking, and available in the colors shown on the surfboard. All trunks have inside coin pocket, panel
supporter. Photo by Tom Kelley at the Hilton Hawaiian Village on recent club outing.

**Actionwear**

*Jantzen, 1966*

Rudi even does dresses to match

**Halter Bra.** Wear it as a bare back halter or convert it to a regular bra. $4.
**Petticoat.** Short for today's short skirts. $4.

**Camise.** A camisole slip with the look of a little chemise. $7.

**Bikini.** Tiny bikini pantie to wear under everything. $2.50.

**Strapless Band Slip.** Y... won't need a bra with t... stretch top band slip. $

Exquisite Form, 1966

Play with
matches
but don't get
burned

Go Gernreich
in the striking
Young Happenings

**Be in Exquisite Form and be what happens.**
Rise and shine in Rudi Gernreich's
"Young Happenings". Matches to go
under whatever you're wearing.
All going together. And one going to
sleep. Go Gernreich in poppies
Get with the with-it
designer. He's what's
happening, baby.

*Look for more
"Young Happenings"
in other kicky prints*

*Sleepwear in 100% cotton.
Lingerie & bras in 50%
Avril® rayon and 50% cotton.
Pantie girdle in 76% nylon
and 24% Lycra®.*

*Exquisite form*®

**Bra.** Rudi's soft little bra. $4. **Bonnie Bra.** New front closing bra. $4. **Bat Wing.** Flying bat-
**i Skant.** Short, short petticoat **Pantie Girdle.** Light and little wing sleeves on this
pantie and garters attached. $7. in a no show length. $8. sleep shortie. $12.

PRICES SLIGHTLY HIGHER IN THE WEST

# SOLARCAINE®
## stops sunburn pain

## ...stops it <u>faster</u>, <u>more</u> <u>completely</u> than ordinary "first aids"

Fiery sunburn doesn't have to spoil your weekend or vacation—for now you can get Solarcaine and *stop the very sensation of pain!*

**First aid for skin pain—all year round!**

Winter *and* summer, Solarcaine stops pain of dozens of skin irritations that hurt, burn, itch—scratches, scrapes, barked shins, cook-out burns, sore feet, even raw cold-weather hands. Sore, blistered lips need Solarcaine Lip Balm.

Solarcaine does *more* than cool your skin instantly. It actually takes the pain out of pain nerves with benzocaine—a surface anesthetic used by doctors. That's why it's much more effective than first aid products that contain no real pain-stopper. And you get many additional reliefs with Solarcaine!

**Helps prevent infection, aids healing**

It moisturizes and softens skin, helps prevent peeling—relieves that parched drawn feeling. Its *antiseptics* medicate your skin, help prevent infection, aid healing.

A unique formula, Solarcaine has brought welcome relief to millions. And it's *greaseless;* white, won't stain. Get Solarcaine today and stop that agonizing sunburn pain fast!

*In smooth-flowing Lotion, handy First Aid Cream, no-touch Spray. Get big saving on large sizes!*

*Quality products of Plough, Inc.*

# WILD, WILD, WILD NEW BEACHGLASSES!

## (and they're polarized!)

Sea & Ski wraps far-out fashion around sensible polarized dark gray lenses. But polarized with Sea & Ski's exclusive new process! It not only filters the light, but also knocks out reflected glare—gives a sharp, clear view with no eyestrain. Come try them all—you'll see! May Co. California Cosmetic Department.

**BOYWATCHERS**
One continuous, flirty peek-hole line curving round your eyes. In Sneaky Pink, Ogle Orange, Snoopy White, Sly Gold, Spy Black, Peeka Blue. $7.95

**DAYTONA**
Wraparounds that corner beautifully with race-car styling! In Black, Dark Olive, Demi-Amber. $4.95

**THUNDERBIRD**
How to make a beautiful take-off with the swept-wing look. In Black, Off-white, Olive, Lemon Yellow. $5.95

**DISCOTHEQUE**
You're framed! Wrapped around with a sleek, chic shadow box in Black, Off-white, Ochre, Olive. $4.95

## MAY CO
California

*May Co California, 1965*

If you're looking for the most luxurious cover-up in the world... don't settle for mink.

## Get Pan-Stik® Make-up only by Max Factor.

With Pan-Stik cream make-up your complexion becomes flawless...quietly elegant. Pan-Stik slips on softly. It covers flaws, covers freckles, covers everything but the beauty of you. It hovers softly on your skin, richer than milk, sweeter than honey to the eye (delicately smooth to the touch). No wonder Pan-Stik is known in certain circles as the make-up that great beauties are made of.

**She just stroked away ten years!**

Dark circles, murky shadows.
Banished with the flick of a finger!
Are you younger?
Of course not.
You just look younger.
Prettier.
Happier.
Alive.
Gone is the stigma of care and years.
Eyes are brighter.
Bigger, too.
It took so little to do so much.
So little to put time in its place.
So little **Powers Crème de la Crème!**

*Powers Crème de la Crème*
ILLUSION OF BEAUTY MAKEUP

# Blonding simplified.

© 1966 CLAIROL INC.

Born Blonde
LOTION LIGHTENER

HAIR LIGHTENING KIT

Clairol announces new Born Blonde® Lightener in its own complete kit. Lifts out dark color faster than anything even Clairol has ever made!

Now blonding is this simple: (1) Lift the dark color out of your hair with new, speeded-up Born Blonde Lightener, in its own we've-thought-of-everything kit.

(2) Shampoo in one of the 12 pale, shimmery shades of Born Blonde, the no-peroxide toner that took the tears out of blonding. Who but Clairol could have done it?

CLAIROL
Born Blonde
LOTION TONER

# If you can't beat'em, join'em.

Any girl so darn sure of herself, she'd wrap her hair about her throat the way she would jewels or furs, you have to hate. Unless, of course, you're that sure of yourself, too.

If you're not, we can give you a little inside dope which you may be able to use to your advantage.

That's not her own hair color. It's ours.

That's Clairol® Creme Toner® No. 9A Towhead® she's used on her pre-lightened hair. (And that's Clairol lip color and make-up just for blondes on her lips and skin.)

Only Clairol Creme Toner gives a girl 32 pale delicate shades to choose from. Which is the reason a Creme Toner shade always seems to belong to the girl wearing it.

Hate is just a big fat waste of time. You, too, can be obnoxiously secure. Join the Clairol Creme Toner blondes.

## The 32 Clairol Creme Toner Blondes

*Clairol, 1969*

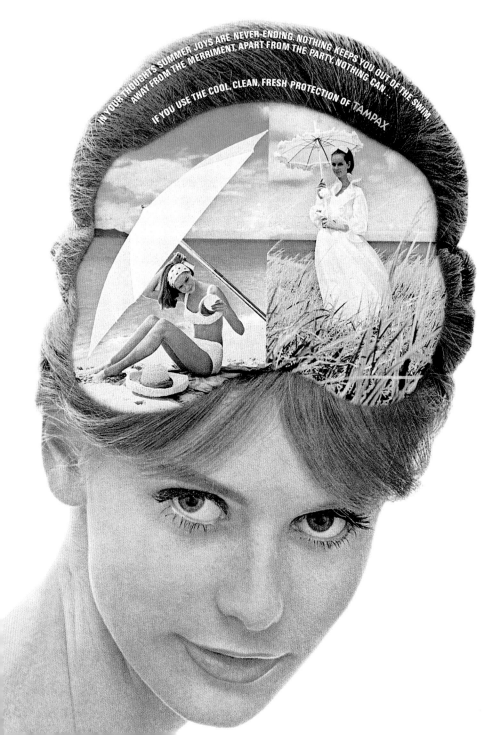

IN YOUR THOUGHTS SUMMER JOYS ARE NEVER-ENDING. NOTHING KEEPS YOU OUT OF THE SWIM, AWAY FROM THE MERRIMENT, APART FROM THE PARTY. NOTHING CAN... IF YOU USE THE COOL, CLEAN, FRESH PROTECTION OF TAMPAX

Bathing suit, Jantzen

## Cares are oceans away

Dress, Artbro

You,
confident,
carefree,
cool,
clean,
fresh,
even on problem days.
Tampax tampons,
worn internally, make
the difference.
This modern sanitary
protection lets you
wear what you wish,
do what you want.

You get
total freedom with

TAMPAX
tampons

TAMPAX TAMPONS ARE MADE ONLY BY
TAMPAX INCORPORATED, PALMER, MASS.

**Maybe the real you...**

# ...is a blonde.

Have you found the real you? Some women never do. In fact, many women never make the most exciting discovery of all: they should have been born blonde. Often a woman who looks merely pleasant with dark hair can be a beauty as a blonde. How about you?

Whether you're a brunette or a blonde whose hair has darkened, it's surprisingly easy today to have pale, shimmering blonde hair – so natural-looking, it even makes you *feel* blonde.

Clairol* has just developed a totally new blonding lotion. The name is Born Blonde,* because that's the way it makes you look.

Will it do the job in 10 minutes? No. But results this flattering and long-lasting are worth some time and care.

First, you or your hairdresser choose the shade that's perfect for you. Next, the dark color is taken out of your hair, with a special lightener. Then your shade of Born Blonde is just poured on!

*No other "permanent" blonding process can change you from dark brunette to pale blonde so simply. And none of those quickie formulas can do it at all. (Honest!)*

Another bonus: because Born Blonde uses no peroxide after the lightening stage, your hair stays shinier and healthier-looking. It may even pick up a little extra glow, from the conditioners in the lotion, and from the light-catching quality of the Born Blonde shades.

Maybe the real you is a blonde. You'll never know until you try.

CLAIROL

Born Blonde

LOTION TONER

Thermo-Jac Model Discoveries, top to bottom: Jan King, Amarillo, Texas; Renee Hollon, Jefferson, Texas; Linda Harris, Waco, Texas; Patricia McNair, Brandon, Miss.

**B. ALTMAN & CO.** New York • **CLARKE'S** Tulsa • **GUS MAYER** New Orleans • **ben SIMON'S** Lincoln • **CAIN SLOAN** Nashville •
**STREETS** Oklahoma City • **WOLF & DESSAUER** Fort Wayne and the Thermo-Jac stores listed on the left.

*Skinny Bones, 1969*

▶ *Coats & Clark, 196*

# Thread, zipper and tape by Coats & Clark.

Before our thread gets on the spool, we test every inch of it over 30 different ways.
That's quality. As for quantity, we make a type of thread for every sewing need you could
possibly think of. And in as many colors. With zipper and tape to match. Because we also
make the only completely coordinated line of accessories. Our 3 Ciel Blue thread matches
our 3 Ciel Blue tape matches our 3 Ciel Blue zipper. Just ask for us by number.
Like they did for Butterick Pattern No. 5250.

# Unfortunately, the trickiest deodorant problem a girl ha isn't under her pretty little arms.

*That* was solved long ago. The real problem, as you very well know, is how to keep the most girl part of you—the vagina. area—fresh and free of any worry-making odors.

Now, finally, there is a way. It's called Pristeen.®

Pristeen is a brand-new vaginal spray deodorant that's been especially developed to cope with the problem.

It works externally, because that's where the trouble starts.

Tension and pressure can cause it. So can getting all hot and perspire-y. So can your own natural body functions. No matter. Whatever starts those troublesome vaginal odors, Pristeen stops them—effectively. And nicely. And very, very gently.

Pristeen has been developed out of intensive research and tested in leading

hospitals under the supervision of gynecologists. While you work your way through long, busy days, it protects you, calmly and quietly, for hours. Pristeen is sure. Completely sure. And it is safe.

Why take chances? Starting today, why not make Pristeen as much a part of your daily life as your bath or shower. It's just as essential to your cleanliness. And to your peace of mind about being a girl.

An attractive, nice-to-be-with girl.

**Nobody's little girl.
Not when you've got a Dune Deck
Tackle Tanky.**

# DUNE DECK

**Swimduds and Sunduds**

Tackle Tanky with polka dot numbers and belt. Of 100% stretch blue C nylon, tested and approved for girls who move. At selectorious stores or write Dune Deck, 1407 Broadway, N.Y.C. 10018, in Canada: 1470 Peel St., Montreal, Quebec. American Dune Deck Sportswear Corp.

Actionwear

*Registered Fabrics Corp., 1967*

Chant d'Arômes is a special way of feeling.

It is the nice way you feel when you love someone and he loves you back.

Or when you breathe in the sweet of a giant forest right after it rains.

Sometimes Chant d'Arômes is a happy feeling.

The feeling you get when a little bird sings a song he made up just for you.

Or when a special person who has been very far away comes home at last.

Chant d'Arômes could be the comfort of having a secret place that is all your very own.

Or having someone understand how you feel, even when you don't tell him.

Chant d'Arômes is lots of things all put together.

Chant d'Arômes is a perfume by Guerlain.

*Chant d'Arômes, 1967*

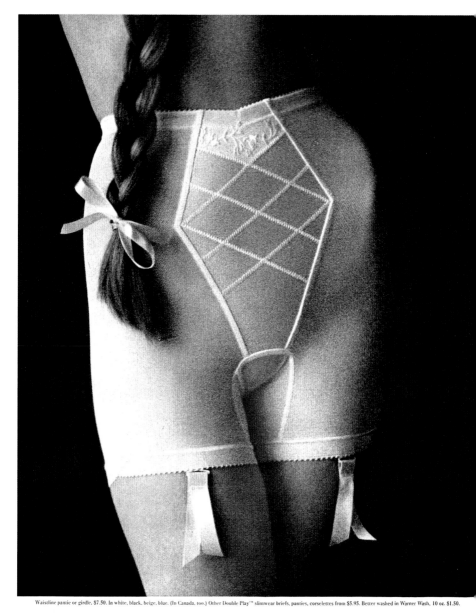

Waistline pantie or girdle, $7.50. In white, black, beige, blue. (In Canada, too.) Other Double Play™ slimwear briefs, panties, corselettes from $5.95. Better washed in Warner Wash, 10 oz. $1.50.

Now there's a girdle with crisscross bands that gives you back the flat tummy of your teens! The Double Play girdle by Warner's®

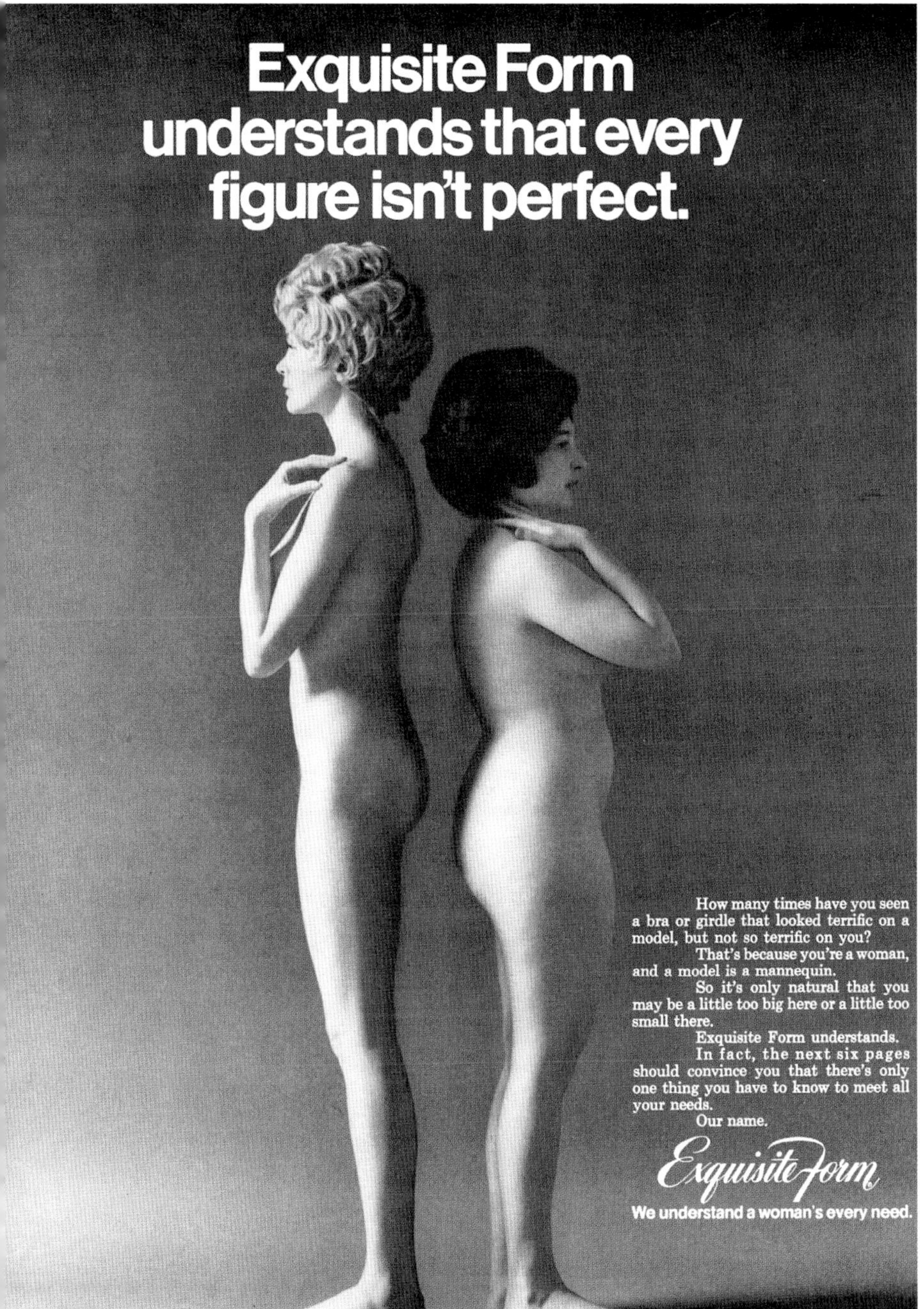


*Exquisite Form, 1969*

# Revlon says:

## This is the year of

# 'The Wild Frosted Wines!'

*A whole new (heavenly!) concept-in-color...*
*muted, mauvey, soft-and-smoky lipshades,*
*low-key, luscious and loaded with frost!*

*These are the elegant off-beats moving in now,*
*changing the mood of mouths (and the total*
*feel of fashion!) as no lipsticks*
*have done in a decade. Soft but bolder.*
*All smoke and smolder. Dusky.*
*Dazzling. Delicious.*

Candied Brandy!

Pink Cognac!

Plum Rum!

*Revlon*
NAIL
ENAMEL

All 3 shades come in loaded-with-frost
lipsticks and Crystalline Nail Enamels.

*Revlon, 1966* ◄

Candied Brandy!

Pink Cognac!

Plum Rum!

The Big Breakaway for Lips and Nails!

# How come all non-conformists look alike?

Maybe it's because the people who select the fashions you'll be wearing think all people who want to be different are the same.

We know better. So we offer you an opportunity to select what you want, not what someone else thinks you want.

And chances are what you select will be different, because it can't be bought in the stores. It can only be sewn.

Every month Simplicity puts out a catalog. The big Simplicity Catalog. It's full of new and newer-than-new fashions.

And if you like, you can make something no one can ever have, except you. Because you choose the patterns and colors and fabrics and trimming. As far-in or as far-out as you like.

We'll be as different as you make us. Which is what makes us different from everyone else.

## Simplicity
Sew your own thing

Simplicity Pattern Co. Inc.
200 Madison Avenue • New York, N.Y. 10016

**DON'T WEAR BILL BLASS DURING THE HUNTING SEASON!**

# Un-nouncing 'Un-Lipstick' by Natural Wonder!

'Un-Lipstick'? It's pale, but the shine won't fail. Bare, but the color's there ( and never, never changes on your lips ). In gleamy little mouthcolors like Ivory Blizzard and Frozen Peaches, Sheer Shiver Pink and Nothing Frosted. 24 shades in all, including the palest frosteds ever put on ice. 'Un-Lipstick'. The liveliest thing that will happen to your lips until you next get kissed.

## Natural Wonder 'Un-Lipstick' by REVLON

# Love him with
# Puritan Ban-Lon® Brookviews
# of DuPont Nylon

Textralized yarn, 100% Du Pont nylon

**Give him America's favorite knit shirts. Full-Fashioned.
Automatic wash and dry. In 25 amorous colors. $8.95 each.**

# PURITAN®
THE PURITAN SPORTSWEAR CORP., 135 W. 50TH ST., NYC

Where to buy it? See last page.

## WHIPPETTE'S RAH-RAH-RAZZLE

It's the Big Game. It's go-team-go. It's the great new dress plays that score on the vervy good looks of Orlon* acrylic. The playoff, left to right, in groups of four: T.E.A.M. SPIRITS—color-paneled with a big "T" or an "E" or an "A" or an "M". Plum, red, blue, green. Each, $23. THE VARSITY SWEATERETTES, low-slung and belty, in red, green, gold, orange. Each, $25. THE FOOTBALL JERSEYS, or how to make sure he gets your number. Green, blue, red, plum. Each, $20. All these Big Game dresses in bonded jersey of 80% "Orlon", 20% wool. Tights, of stretch Du Pont nylon. Orange, gold, red, green, plum. S.M. $4.

# Take a stand on platforms!

# We did!

Give our new platforms a try.
They're fashion's exciting new High-Ri
Designed to give your look a new
lift. A bolder stance. A broader heel.
Greater footing—with lots of sole.
Escape the last-year look. Come see our collecti
of all-new, all-now platforms. At most Sears,
Roebuck and Co. stores.

**The Shoe Place at**

**Sears**

the fashion stop

# When it's time for sportswear you look smarter and feel better in

## JARMAN *Casuals*

About $14.00

J2593

J2592

J2093

J2591

J2594

Best foundation for your sportswear wardrobe? A pair of Jarman casuals—easily! Built for comfort, styled with nonchalant distinction, colorful as all outdoors. (Though naturally comfortable, Jarman casuals—like all Jarman styles—are "wear-tested" to assure you more comfort and better fit. This means that every original model, before being approved for production, is extensively worn under everyday conditions.) See your dealer's selection of these colorful, comfortable Jarmans. You'll want a pair for each of your sportswear outfits.

*Available at Jarman dealers and stores from coast to coast.*
*(We also make Jarman Jrs. for boys.)*

## Jarman
### SHOES FOR MEN

JARMAN SHOE COMPANY · NASHVILLE, TENNESSEE 37202 · A DIVISION OF GENESCO ®

Each style shown, about $14.00. Other Jarman casual styles from $12.00 to $16.00. (Prices slightly higher in the West.)

JARMAN CASUALS COME IN THIS WIDE ARRAY OF COLORS

# The "in" hairfashions that go on when you go out.

**CONTESSA WIG**
Pre-Styled in the latest Paris hair fashion. Superbly crafted of 100% human hair.

**CAMEO CLASSIC Curly Top Wiglet**
The young look of ringlets adds a fashion flair to short and long hair. Of genuine David/L®.

**CAMEO PONYTAIL**
Wear it swinging at discotheques . . . pin it up when going chic! Of genuine David/L®.

**CROWNING GLORY Pouf Curls Wiglet**
Wear it elaborate for evening . . . casual for day—Expertly crafted of 100% human hair

Go casual one minute. Go glamorous the next. Pick the look you'd like to have and a David & David hairpiece will create it for you of natural human hair or real David/L® . . . easily, instantly! Wigs, Demi-Wigs, Chignons, Wiglets, Postiches, Ponytails, Pouf Curls, Drop Curls . . . salon-styled coiffures to give you an in-fashion look for every occasion. Wear one . . . start a collection! At fine stores everywhere.

Fashionably "in" wigs and hairpieces by

## David & David

David and David, Inc., Long Island City, New York
World's Largest Manufacturers of Quality Hair Products for Over 50 Years

Cut up, cut out, cut loose with Max Factor's

# CALIFORNIA PINK·A·PADES

**Two pink escapades for lips and fingertips.
Two sheer...two shimmering...too tempting!**

It's the great new color adventure for summer.
Say it Pink-A-Pale (soft, feminine, fragile)
or Pink-A-Fling (lively, zingy, daring).
Wear it either super-sheer or super-frosted.
Any way you play it, have a wild
pink Pink-A-Pade!

*Max Factor, 1967*

# Even the prettiest hairdo
## won't make up for a bad complexion

Mmm! Your new hairdo is a real pretty-pretty. But you're finding out that even the cutest flip can flop if you've got bumps and blemishes.

**Brush those tears away!** Today you can start the proven skin care that works wonders to give you a clearer, prettier complexion! It's easier than you think—with Noxzema Skin Cream. America's leading medicated cream has helped millions of girls clear up teen age skin problems. Follow this easy Noxzema routine and don't miss a single day!

**Every morning and night,** wash your face with Noxzema. It cleans like soap, but doesn't dry your skin. It's greaseless—so it washes off with water! Medicates surface blemishes as it cleans.

**Smooth Noxzema on under make-up.** It works invisibly all day to help clear those blemishes.

**At night,** after washing, put a little extra Noxzema on spots and blemishes. Five medicinal ingredients help clear them up fast. And it's greaseless—won't stain your pillow.

Start today! See how regular Noxzema care helps keep skin clear—helps stop trouble before it starts.

**Now—Noxzema LIQUID Skin Cream**—if you love to use a liquid. Same famous Noxzema medication —same greaseless formula—same lovely results!

*Noxzema, 1966*

# No-no's.
## for mommies
### from Winnie-the-Pooh

No untidiness

No ironing

No bagging

No mismatches

No money down on Sears revolving charge

No doubt about it! Pooh's new red, white and blue fashions for Spring are positively great.

They're color-coordinated so they mix and match beautifully. (It's easy for kids to dress themselves without clashing.)

Pooh's durable PERMA-PREST® and stretch nylon fashions are easy for you, too. Tumble dry and no ironing ever. No untidiness or bagging either.

Pooh offers classical styling, long wear and built-in mothers' helpers—all at Sears reasonable prices (so they're easy on mommies' budgets, too).

Remember, extra work for yourself is a no-no. So let Pooh bear the burden—with children's fashions from Sears, Roebuck and Co.

The Winnie-the-Pooh Collection only at

### Sears

© Walt Disney Productions
MCMLXIV

**out of one pattern a whole wardrobe grows and grows with Penney's variety of wash 'n wear\***

## regulated cottons

Pick from fields of flower prints...infinite geometrics ...a world of colors wonderful as a child's imagination ... all exclusively Penney's. Sew these beautifully behaved fabrics into fashions, so crease-resistant they stay unruffled through hours of sitting at the desk, lively recess tussles. *Machine-washable, minimum ironing ... Sanforized® against shrinkage...designed to add new beauty to every minute of her young life.   *all, 36 inches wide.*

79¢ yard

*Lazy-Bones, 1966*

Blazers are the new casuals that make it exciting to do nothing at all. Styled wild and turned on with color. From subtlest tones to craziest pastels. Lazy looking but built to take it... like all Bostonian fine-crafted shoes. Blazers are cushion soft and so flexible they're better than barefoot. So smart they'll go anywhere in style. So when you take to the hills, or the beach, or the big game, take your walk on the wild side. In new **Bostonian Blazers.**

# Introducing Bostonian Blazers:
# A walk on the wild side.

9628 TEXAS GOLD

9604 FOREST GREEN

9626 WILLOW GREEN

9624 DENIM BLUE

9602 SAND

BOSTONIAN BLAZERS. SUN 'N FUN CASUALS, FROM $14.95 (SLIGHTLY HIGHER IN THE WEST.) WRITE
FOR NAME OF NEAREST BOSTONIAN BLAZER DEALER, BOSTONIAN SHOES, WHITMAN, MASSACHUSETTS

*Bostonian Blazers, 1967*

THE
MADNESS
OF
COTTON
*as expressed by Adele Simpson*
Great, colorful flowers that explode like fireworks
in a white, white firmament. Cotton made it happen. Cotton
made it the high fashion it is. Wear it and
listen for the murmurs of admiration, the sighs of envy.
*National Cotton Council, Box 12285,*
*Memphis, Tenn. 38112.*

COMFORTABLE · CAREFREE
COTTON

*National Cotton Council, 1967*

## THE COMPATIBILITY OF COTTON

*as expressed by Tarquin for Samuel Robert*
You go with cotton because cotton goes with everything.
See how it goes with leather. See how the natural
beauty of leather goes with the natural beauty of cotton.
Tarquin of Samuel Robert saw, then designed
this dress and coat ensemble. What will they think
of next? With cotton, there's no telling.
*National Cotton Council, Box 12285,*
*Memphis, Tennessee 38112.*

COMFORTABLE · CAREFREE
**COTTON**

Be honey.
Be heady.
Be here and now.
But be sure. Sure as
new Kotex napkins–
now with deep-downy
Soft-Impressions!

THE FINEST FEMININE PROTECTION COMES FROM KIMBERLY-CLARK

GOWN BY JON HAGGINS—JEWELRY SANT' ANGELO

New centers of softness·in Kotex® napkins absorb faster, protect better.

**Break out of your little girl body when you're feeling in a big girl mood.**

Be more woman in our unique Mabs bra.

REMEMBER WHEN STRETCH WAS JUST ANOTHER WORD? NOW IN CELANESE NYLON

# *fashion-stretch*

**Sea B, Inc.** puts new spirit in swimwear with Fashion-Stretch, the exciting fabric that keeps pace with every move. Shadows your shape, and keeps its own lastingly. In Edmos' knit of Celanese Nylon. Two-piece suit, ringed at midriff. Tobacco and orange, blue and olive, gold and black. High-necked maillot with back halter strap. Tobacco and orange, plum and lime, blue and cocoa. Each, 30 to 36, about $20. At Franklin Simon, New York; L. S. Ayres & Co., Indiana; Bamberger's New Jersey; The Hecht Co., Baltimore; Joseph Magnin Co., California & Nevada.

Celanese®

**FASHION STRETCH OF**  **CELANESE nYLON**
Add a fiber from Celanese and good things get better

TM OF CHEMSTRAND FOR APPROVED STRETCH APPAREL

**What do you wear under Actionwear?**　　　　　**Actionwear Underwear.**

Sears has it. The first inside-outside Actionwear* outfit for juniors. Including the new Actionwear bra and panty girdle. The Actionwear underwear is made with Chemstrand Blue "C"® spandex. This means you get great comfort plus control. Smoothline seam-free cup bra with stretchy straps, sizes A and B, 32 to 36. About $5. Design-in-Motion® panty Girdle, with mesh inserts in back for extra give, 5-15 (junior

sizes). About $6. Now you're ready for Actionwear pants (100% stretch Blue "C"® nylon) and Actionwear top (50% polyester/50% stretch Blue "C"® nylon). Top, S-M-L (junior sizes) about $5. Pants 5-13, about $9. Also in loden and pale blue. And all tagged Actionwear, the very best in stretch clothes. Tested and approved by Chemstrand. So run right now to Sears, Roebuck and Co. That's where the Action is for juniors.

Actionwear
The very best in stretch clothes

CHEMSTRAND, N.Y. 10001, A DIVISION OF Monsanto

# This is no shape for a girl.

## hat's why Warner's makes the Concentrate girdle and the Little Fibber bra.

Girls with too much bottom and too little top: rner's® can reshape you.

We reshape you on the bottom with the Con-trate girdle: Its all-around panels do more you than a little girdle (they're lined up to p you where you need help most), yet Con-trate doesn't squash you like a heavy girdle.

We reshape your top with the Little Fibber bra. The super-soft fiberfill lining doesn't make a big production out of you. It rounds out your bosom just enough to go with your trimmed-down hips.

All of a sudden, you've got a proportioned body, and your clothes fit better. Warner's calls this a Body-Do.™ You can get fitted for one in any good store.

ODY-DO FOR THE AVERAGE PEAR: THE LITTLE FIBBER™ CONTOUR BRA, $3. THE CONCENTRATE™ GIRDLE, $12. WARNER SLIMWEAR-LINGERIE. A DIVISION OF THE WARNER BROTHERS COMPANY

the panty hose
created specially
for teens
Eye-catchers
PANTY HOSE
The shorter skirts are for you. Show off your legs and not your stocking tops in the smartest panty hose made for teens. No girdling. No gartering. Berkshire styling. Berkshire quality.
only $2.00 a pair
BERKSHIRE
INTERNATIONAL

Sears has gone wild!

# The Sun Fighter

Bronze Lustre's the name. Protects you while you tan soft, tan deep, tan smooth. Fights sun-damage, sun-aging with an exclusive Revlon sunscreen. And it's loaded with special moisturizers; acts like a night cream in the sun to guard against sun dryness and wrinkles.

Two formulas: Regular and Extra-protective, both in gelée, lotion or foam. And for your lips —Bronze Lustre Sun Sticks in Pink Gloss, Peach Gloss, Tan Gloss, Coral Gloss, Natural Gloss.

**New! Bronze Lustre After Sun Silk** – to sleek on all over at sundown. It moisturizes, softens and smooths; helps prevent flaking and peeling. Makes even a little tan look like a lot.

So go ahead. Expose those wide open spaces. Bronze Lustre's got you covered all the way.

*Revlon*
'Bronze
Lustre'
Tanning Gelée

# Wear St. Johns and be on the side of the angels.

## St. Johns Cologne, the lime of least resistance.

. Johns Lime Cologne. Imported from the West Indies. Crisp. Invigorating. With a subtle, lingering fragrance that has caused many an angel to fall.
St. Johns Lime Cologne, $5.00; Lime After Shave, $4.00. Also Available: St. Johns Lime Soap, Deodorant, Talc, Moisturizer and Gift Sets.

# Join the tan-ables... get the best of the sun

Co-starring in Martin Ransohoff's "Don't Make Waves" says

Coppertone is a reg. TM of Plough, I
Also available in Canada.

# "Coppertone gives you a *better* tan"

## *(—it's enriched to give extra protection, too!)*

You *do* get a better tan with Coppertone. The fastest tan possible with maximum sunburn protection . . . plus extra safeguards against skin dryness. Coppertone contains the most widely beach-tested sunscreen. It's also enriched with lanolin, cocoa butter and other moisturizers that make your skin more tan-able . . . keep your skin soft and satiny sleek.

So join the tan-ables. Get a better tan . . . deep, dark, superbly smooth. Coppertone outsells them all because it out-tans them all! Get the best of the sun with enriched Coppertone. Save on large size.

Don't be a paleface!

**TAN, DON'T BURN**—*with America's most popular, most complete line of suntan products: Lotion, Oil, Cream, Spray, Shade®, Noskote®, Lipkote®, Royal Blend®. Also new, Baby Tan® for young children and Royal Blend Soap.*

# Leslie Hornby
# found someone
# she can lean on

Max Factor predicts: Spring will be a littl

# the Sun Sheers

# DAMSEL IN UNDRESS!

**The escape from ordinary everyday underthings?** In the hurry-up put-on of the striking white lace-trimmed bra-chemise culotte of Caprolan®, the nylon that takes color better. 32-36 A and B, 34-38 C. About $5. Style #3219. Also striking white again as a matching slip at about $4.50. Style #3119. At fine stores. Write 392 Fifth Ave., New York, N.Y. 10018. **Movie Star**

Mavest, 1968 ◄

Cotton Producers Institute, 1968

# Isn't that Raquel Welch behind those Foster Grants?

(Yes indeed. See her in "Bandolero," from 20th Century Fox.)

To remove any further speculation, we'll own up. That is Miss Welch.

But, as you can see, our Foster Grants (known to many as the Sunglasses of the Stars) have done it again. They've given Raquel a new dimension. Several in fact.

One moment she's capricious. Then contented. Now candid. Even coy.

That, kind heart, is the Spell of the Shades.

Long, long ago folks wore sunglasses only when they were under the sun. Now they wear them from sun up till sun up. From New Year's Day till New Year's Eve.

In every kind of weather. Everywhere.

Sunglasses have become funglasses.

We can't tell you how happy that makes us, since Foster Grant is clearly the leader in the anti-glare business.

We have more styles in more colors than anybody.

And they all have ff77 lenses that meet U.S. Government standards for eye protection (standards a lot of expensive imports don't meet).

Now, if somebody mentioned sunglasses, who would you think of first?

Besides Raquel Welch.

"Am I doomed, C. B., to play the sex symbol in an age of flower children?"

"So you admit you didn't come to Zermatt just to climb the Matterhorn."

". . . and now, love, you know all my secrets."

"If you really wanted to hang on to Rhodesia, Sir Robert, why didn't you tell me?"

"Any man who straightens his tie as often as you just has to be hiding something."

"Matador, you're looking at a woman who wants more than a moment of truth."

Join the movers. Doing their own thing with the Runarounds.
A flash of color. A glint of metal. Wrapping around for a smashing good loo[k]
If you still call them sunglasses you're missing all the fashion.
At fine stores everywhere.

## Riviera®

*Trevira, 1968*

**MAVEST** shapes the sports coats to have in The Trevira Era. In fabric as emphatically individual as the jackets themselves. Firm-bodied, infinitely adaptable to the new demands of today's living. In 55% Trevira® polyester, 45% wool. The Gurkha tunic, smooth, crisp, lean. The double-breasted blazer, essential for the city-country man. And the side-vented, two button blazer. Each about $55 at stores that know what a man wants now, in The Trevira Era. Hystron Fibers Incorporated, 485 Lexington Ave., New York 10017

**TREVIRA**
The Extraordinary Fiber

# THE TREVIRA ERA

The beginning of something extraordinary in America.

# "If you don't give him 007 ...I will"

Now, dare to give him what he really wants—007, the bold new grooming aids that make any man dangerous.

There's a 007 gift set for every assignment. The arsenal includes 007 After Shave, Hair Tonic, Spray Deodorant, Cologne, Shave Cream, Talc and Soap. Each has the license to kill...women.

Give him as much as you dare. But hurry. If you don't, someone else will.

The full line:
All seven 007 grooming aids, $9.00

For special assignments:
007 After Shave, Cologne, Talc, Shave Cream, $5.50

When he's traveling light:
007 After Shave and Cologne, $3.50

*007 Parfume, 1965*

▶ *Hathaway, 1968*

# ARE YOU READY FOR CENTAUR?

## it's the Massage Cologne ...half man, half beast, all male!

Out of the Wild and Violent days of ancient Greece comes the exciting concept of a Massage Cologne...it's name is CENTAUR.

Each morning...each evening massage CENTAUR into your torso.

Massage CENTAUR into your arms, legs, and loins.

CENTAUR has *no alcohol* to irritate, so it massages with comfort into sensitive areas.

CENTAUR adds a delightful new dimension to your body, a low level aroma that hovers close to the skin for hours, transmits its virile message only in moments of close and intimate contact.

CENTAUR makes no coy promises...finding HER is up to you...then CENTAUR gives HER the message. She won't say, "What are you wearing?" She will say, *"You smell good!"*

© 1967 Century Creations, Inc., P. O. Box 1499, Santa Monica, Calif.

Introductory
Collectors CLASSIC – 8 oz.......... **$10.00**
(Rugged unglazed porcelain, 24K gold finish)
REFILL SET–8 oz. & dispenser pump **$6.50**
TRIAL SIZE – ½ oz................... **$1.00**

TREASURE CHEST $10.00

# "My men wear English Leather or they wear nothing at all."

I know men.
I've grown up with them all about me.
And I like men.
But some are a lot more persuasive than others.
I think the way they smell has a lot to do with it.
So I don't take any chances.
I give my men English Leather® every chance I get.

BUCCANEER
$5.75

PADDOCK
$4.50

## All she wants is a little Emotion

*(a lot of it if she's daring!)*

Emotion...
the new perfume
born in France...
translated in America
into Perfume Spray,
Eau de Parfum,
Eau de Parfum Mist,
Dusting Powder,
Perfume and Bath Oil.
Prices from
3.00 to 17.50.

## Emotion
by
## Helena Rubinstein

*Available at fine cosmetic counters everywhere.*

EMOTION

EMOTION
EAU DE PARFUM MIST

HELENA
RUBINSTEIN®

© 1965, Helena Rubinstein, Inc.

# What makes dancing
# a contact sport again?

## Passport™ 360
## by Van Heusen

When a man wears
Passport 360, there's
no way to dance
but close. No place
to be but near him.
No way to act but
wild. Cologne from
$3.50. After Shave
from $3. Spray Deodorant
from $2.50. Now in special
holiday gift sets.
You can go as far as you
like...with Passport 360

*McCall's Patterns, 1964*

FACCIONE

Sammy is particular.
He knows we don't manufacture suits.
  We make them. Much the way a Savile
Row tailor makes his.

  Mostly by hand.
  We hand-cut the cloth.
  Then we shape it. And baste it.
  And sew it. And button-hole it.
By hand.
  In all, we put an average of 40% more
hand-shaping into our suits than you'll find
in other suits that cost as much. Or more.
  Why?
  Because it's the only way to be sure
that the suit will fit. Precisely.
  So when a friend asks Sammy
who his tailor is, he tells them.

### GROSHIRE/AUSTIN LEEDS
GROSSMAN CLOTHING CO. INC., 1290 AVENUE OF THE AMERICAS, N.Y. 10019.

## When they ask Sammy about his Nehru suit, he tells them he had it made. And he's not putting them on.

*Revlon, 1969*

Mitsouko by Guerlain

if she doesn't give it to you, get it yourself!

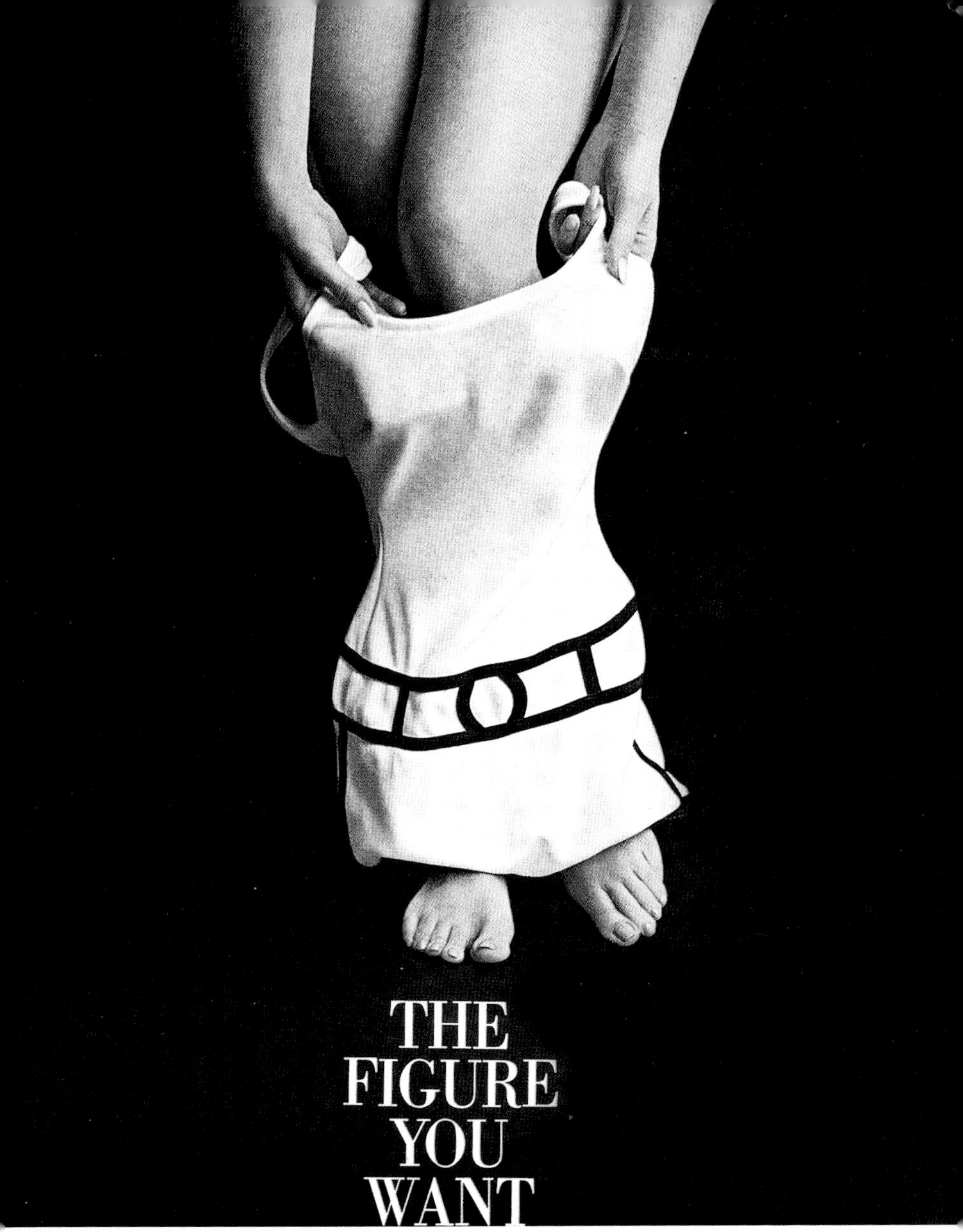

THE
FIGURE
YOU
WANT
IS IN EVERY
PETER PAN® SWIMSUIT
OF NYLON & ORLON®

FONT'S REG. T.M.    PRICES SLIGHTLY HIGHER IN FLORIDA AND THE WEST.

eter Pan's exclusive "Custom Cup"™ Swim Bra combines world-famous Hidden Treasure® and atural Treasure™ bras. The first self-adjusting bra in a swimsuit. Fits the way you want it to, hether you're A, B, C, or in-between. A great example: our terrific "Band Dandy" **designed by eg Cassini.** At these stores and branches: B. Altman & Co., New York; Carson, Pirie Scott & Co., Chicago; Shillito's, Cincinnati; Sanger-Harris, Dallas; odward & Lothrop, Washington, D.C. The figure you want is in every Peter Pan swimsuit, bra and girdle. One piece boy leg of double knit stretch in Du Pont on and Orlon* acrylic. In white with black, yellow with black, or navy with white. 8 to 16, about $24. One piece classic, 10 to 16, about $26. Two-piece hipster, 8 to 14, ut $24. Peter Pan Swimwear International, Inc., 1407 Broadway, New York 10018. In Canada: 7585 St. Lawrence Blvd., Montreal 10, Quebec.

Oh go ahead! You know you'd love to try it. Gold lipstick

Frosted
Gone Gold

Frosted
Fool's Gold

Frosted
Spanish Gold

If Mother Nature is so smart
why weren't we *born* with go'
Just like mine. And *frosted* to
And creamy. And in three
frosted Coty Cremestick sha'
Oh, well. I guess Coty
has to think of everything.

Cremestick
Coty

# THE
# 10-MINUTE
## (between shampoo)
# SET

Your dryer
turns it on!
Honest!

**Lektro Set**
*Toni*

## lektro set.
### and the heat from your dryer
### turn on a new set <u>between</u> <u>shampoos</u>.

Just a day or two since you shampooed,
and your hair is a put-down. Limp.
Lifeless. Straggly. Now, just ten minutes under
a dryer can turn on a fresh, bouncy set!
New Lektro Set, the ten-minute heat setting spray, turns
on a holding set between shampoos! Set your
dry hair strand by strand with Lektro Set. In just
ten-minutes, the heat from your dryer turns
on the special "between shampoos" holding ingredients
in Lektro Set. You'll brush out the softest,
holdingest set you ever got from dry hair!
Try new Lektro Set, by Toni. It can change a put-down
to a turn-on in just ten minutes!

**70s Fashion**
Ed. Jim Heimann / Flexi-cover,
192 pp. / € 6.99 / $ 9.99 /
£ 4.99 / ¥ 1.500

**Fashion Now 2**
Eds. Terry Jones, Susie Rushton /
Flexi-cover, 640 pp. / € 29.99 /
$ 39.99 / £ 19.99 / ¥ 5.900

**All-American Ads 1900-1919**
Steven Heller / Ed. Jim Heimann /
Flexi-cover, 640 pp. / € 29.99 /
$ 39.99 / £ 19.99 / ¥ 5.900

# "These books are beautiful objects, well-designed and lucid." —*Le Monde*, Paris, on the ICONS series

## " Buy them all and add some pleasure to your life."

**60s Fashion**
Ed. Jim Heimann

**70s Fashion**
Ed. Jim Heimann

**African Style**
Ed. Angelika Taschen

**Alchemy & Mysticism**
Alexander Roob

**American Indian**
Dr. Sonja Schierle

**Angels**
Gilles Néret

**Architecture Now!**
Ed. Philip Jodidio

**Art Now**
Eds. Burkhard Riemschneider,
Uta Grosenick

**Atget's Paris**
Ed. Hans Christian Adam

**Bamboo Style**
Ed. Angelika Taschen

**Ingrid Bergman**
Ed. Paul Duncan, Scott Eyman

**Berlin Style**
Ed. Angelika Taschen

**Humphrey Bogart**
Ed. Paul Duncan, James Ursini

**Marlon Brando**
Ed. Paul Duncan,
F.X. Feeney

**Brussels Style**
Ed. Angelika Taschen

**Cars of the 50s**
Ed. Jim Heimann,
Tony Thacker

**Cars of the 60s**
Ed. Jim Heimann, Tony Thacker

**Cars of the 70s**
Ed. Jim Heimann, Tony Thacker

**Charlie Chaplin**
Ed. Paul Duncan, David Robinson

**China Style**
Ed. Angelika Taschen

**Christmas**
Ed. Jim Heimann, Steven Heller

**Design Handbook**
Charlotte & Peter Fiell

**Design for the 21ˢᵗ Century**
Eds. Charlotte & Peter Fiell

**Design of the 20ᵗʰ Century**
Eds. Charlotte & Peter Fiell

**Marlene Dietrich**
Ed. Paul Duncan,
James Ursini

**Devils**
Gilles Néret

**Robert Doisneau**
Ed. Jean-Claude Gautrand

**East German Design**
Ralf Ulrich/Photos: Ernst Hedler

**Clint Eastwood**
Ed. Paul Duncan, Douglas
Keesey

**Egypt Style**
Ed. Angelika Taschen

**Encyclopaedia Anatomica**
Ed. Museo La Specola Florence

**M.C. Escher**

**Fashion**
Ed. The Kyoto Costume Institute

**Fashion Now!**
Eds. Terry Jones, Susie Rushton

**Fruit**
Ed. George Brookshaw,
Uta Pellgrü-Gagel

**HR Giger**
HR Giger

**Grand Tour**
Harry Seidler

**Cary Grant**
Ed. Paul Duncan, F.X. Feeney

**Graphic Design**
Eds. Charlotte & Peter Fiell

**Greece Style**
Ed. Angelika Taschen

**Halloween**
Ed. Jim Heimann,
Steven Heller

**Havana Style**
Ed. Angelika Taschen

**Audrey Hepburn**
Ed. Paul Duncan, F.X. Feeney

**Katharine Hepburn**
Ed. Paul Duncan, Alain Silver

**Homo Art**
Gilles Néret

**Hot Rods**
Ed. Coco Shinomiya, Tony
Thacker

**Hula**
Ed. Jim Heimann

**India Bazaar**
Samantha Harrison, Bari Kumar

**London Style**
Ed. Angelika Taschen

**Steve McQueen**
Ed. Paul Duncan, Alain Silver

**Mexico Style**
Ed. Angelika Taschen

**Miami Style**
Ed. Angelika Taschen

**Minimal Style**
Ed. Angelika Taschen

**Marilyn Monroe**
Ed. Paul Duncan,
F.X. Feeney

**Morocco Style**
Ed. Angelika Taschen

**New York Style**
Ed. Angelika Taschen

**Paris Style**
Ed. Angelika Taschen

**Penguin**
Frans Lanting

**20ᵗʰ Century Photography**
Museum Ludwig Cologne

**Pierre et Gilles**
Eric Troncy

**Provence Style**
Ed. Angelika Taschen

**Robots & Spaceships**
Ed. Teruhisa Kitahara

**Safari Style**
Ed. Angelika Taschen

**Seaside Style**
Ed. Angelika Taschen

**Signs**
Ed. Julius Wiedeman

**South African Style**
Ed. Angelika Taschen

**Starck**
Philippe Starck

**Surfing**
Ed. Jim Heimann

**Sweden Style**
Ed. Angelika Taschen

**Tattoos**
Ed. Henk Schiffmacher

**Tiffany**
Jacob Baal-Teshuva

**Tokyo Style**
Ed. Angelika Taschen

**Tuscany Style**
Ed. Angelika Taschen

**Valentines**
Ed. Jim Heimann,
Steven Heller

**Web Design: Best Studios**
Ed. Julius Wiedemann

**Web Design: Best Studios 2**
Ed. Julius Wiedemann

**Web Design: E-Commerce**
Ed. Julius Wiedemann

**Web Design: Flash Sites**
Ed. Julius Wiedemann

**Web Design: Music Sites**
Ed. Julius Wiedemann

**Web Design: Portfolios**
Ed. Julius Wiedemann

**Orson Welles**
Ed. Paul Duncan,
F.X. Feeney

**Women Artists**
**in the 20th and 21st Century**
Ed. Uta Grosenick

★
ICONS